The
BEATING OCD
Workbook

Dr Stephanie Fitzgerald

Dedicated to James Matthew Taylor (Baby James).
Quite simply, the best nephew in the world.

The BEATING OCD Workbook

Dr Stephanie Fitzgerald

First published in Great Britain in 2014 by Hodder and Stoughton. An Hachette UK company.

First published in US in 2014 by The McGraw-Hill Companies, Inc.

This edition published in 2014 by Hodder and Stoughton

British Library Cataloguing in Publication Data: a catalogue record for this title is available from the British Library.

Library of Congress Catalog Card Number: on file.

Paperback ISBN 978 1 473 60134 5

10 9 8 7 6 5 4 3 2 1

Cover image © Thinkstock images

Typeset by Cenveo Publisher Services.

Printed and bound in Great Britain by CPI Group (UK) Ltd., Croydon, CR0 4YY.

Hodder and Stoughton policy is to use papers that are natural, renewable and recyclable products and made from wood grown in sustainable forests. The logging and manufacturing processes are expected to conform to the environmental regulations of the country of origin.

Hodder and Stoughton

338 Euston Road

London NW1 3BH

www.hodder.co.uk

Acknowledgments

I would like to thank Ashley Fulwood, Chief Executive of OCD-UK, for his continuing encouragement and support. Ashley is incredibly selfless with his time and energy and works tirelessly to support those affected by OCD. I am forever grateful for all his help and encouragement with my research. I hope he knows the huge difference he makes to those dealing with OCD.

I would also like to acknowledge Diana Wilson and Maria Bavetta, who co-founded the charity Maternal OCD. They identified an essential area of OCD that needed recognition, promotion and normalizing and they have worked so hard to increase awareness and reduce stigma – bravo ladies!

Thank you to everyone who responded to my request for ideas. I wanted to make this book as useful as possible and so I appealed for those affected by OCD to tell me what they most wanted to read in this book. Every suggestion has made it into the book and I so appreciate your ideas and suggestions. Thank you.

I would like to thank all my patients, who have worked with me and successfully overcome their OCD.

Last, but definitely not least, I want to thank my family and my friends. Your ongoing support means the world to me and I love you all lots.

Contents

1

How to use this workbook

→ ## What can I expect from each chapter?

This book is divided into chapters, which contain a mixture of information and exercises. The idea of having a workbook, as opposed to a textbook, is that you read through and understand the theory behind the therapy, and then get an opportunity to practise the skills you have just learned. Follow the book in chapter order and you will build on previously gained knowledge and be able to make sense of how OCD works and how best to overcome it. It may be tempting to skip to the chapters that feel the most relevant to your OCD and ignore the rest. However, in doing so you will not be building on your understanding, and references to topics covered in previous chapters won't make much sense, so do ensure that you read the book in order from start to finish.

→ ## What do I need to complete the exercises?

When working through this workbook you will need the following:

A THERAPY NOTEBOOK

Your Therapy Notebook is where you can make notes on what you have learned but also a place to jot down your own thoughts, reactions and reflections on your journey out of OCD. It is important to keep track of your progress in this way.

Often we can become so focused on our end goal that we forget to look back and acknowledge all the progress we have made so far. The

Therapy Notebook helps you to keep track of progress and can provide valuable motivation when times are tough, or you need an extra boost to get you to the next stage. You may choose to keep your notes on your phone, tablet or laptop but often it is easier to track our thoughts by hand. A Therapy Notebook has been included at the end of this book so that you can keep your thoughts and notes together with the information and exercises in this book.

TIME AND SPACE

You need to dedicate time to complete the exercises and this includes having a space where you can think uninterrupted. Although we all lead busy lives these days, the exercises have been designed to fit in with everyday living. Therefore it may be a case of finding an extra 15 minutes in your day just for you to focus on working through this book.

SUPPORT

Therapy of any type can be challenging and it is useful to have some support. Whether that's from a professional (e.g. letting your GP know) or whether it's from a trusted friend or colleague, it is good to have support and encouragement.

REWARDS

I'm a huge fan of rewards. I don't understand why we ever grow out of them! We reward children with treats, sticker charts and pocket money so why do we deprive ourselves as adults? Rewards can be extremely motivating and can give an extra boost when our energy is flagging. You are taking a brave step in overcoming your OCD so line up some treats and rewards for yourself as you go. A little boost can go a long way and can make you more likely to stick with the task.

→ My OCD makes it hard to read books. How can I manage this?

For some people, OCD can make reading a struggle. Perhaps you re-read chapters again and again or perhaps you find your mind is too agitated and you worry you are not taking in the key points. My advice would be to record, either in your notebook (mentioned above, and with an blank example near the end of the book) or on a dictaphone/smartphone, any key points that you would like to remember. This way you can identify them without having to read through the whole chapter again and you can listen to them whenever you want to.

This is a technique I often use in therapy with individuals who worry about retaining the key points covered in sessions, and it relieves the pressure of committing everything to memory.

Also, this book is written in my voice and my style and that may not be the easiest way to remember key bits of information. Often it is much easier to form our own 'memory tags' or ways of remembering points in our own words. I would encourage you to record these as well. If something makes sense but you struggle to remember it, then rephrase it in your own voice, or with your own explanation, making it easier to remember.

Another technique would be to keep your notepad and pen beside you as you read and then if a persistent thought or distraction comes into your head then just make a note of it and continue reading. This ensures that you won't forget whatever it is that you have just thought of, and leaves your mind free to focus on your reading.

Hopefully, these techniques will help you overcome the difficulties that OCD can cause when we are trying to concentrate and focus while reading.

→ Who should read this book?

This book is aimed at those who are interested in learning about, and practising, some CBT (Cognitive Behavioural Therapy) techniques to help them overcome their OCD symptoms. Therefore this book would be useful for anyone affected by OCD, including those living with someone with OCD. There is no doubt that OCD is a disorder that affects those around the person with OCD – in fact in a very short period of time OCD can become a 'family affair'. As such I would encourage the friends, family or carers (FFC) of someone with OCD to read through this book as well. This will hopefully provide some explanations of the way OCD works and how best FFC can respond to the OCD.

→ I've heard a lot about CBT (Cognitive Behavioural Therapy) – is this my only option?

If CBT has been recommended to you, or you have been thinking about CBT for a while, then this book may be helpful. While it is in no way designed to replace one-to-one therapy, it may provide a useful introduction to the ideas and techniques that you would experience in a one-to-one therapy situation. This will allow you to 'get a feel' for CBT and whether this is an approach that suits you.

CBT is not your only option when it comes to therapy as there are a great many models of therapy and different approaches available. However, CBT has by far the greatest evidence base for the treatment of OCD, and it is the approach recommended by the National Institute for Health and Care Excellence (NICE).

You can find a link to the NICE guidelines for treatment for OCD under the 'Useful contacts' section of this book.

→ I'm reading this book for someone else – how can I use it to help them?

There are suggestions throughout this book for individuals living with someone with a diagnosis/those who want to help. Unfortunately, we cannot make someone else better. Individuals need to choose when the time is right for them to make some changes happen and they need to want to change. However, making them aware of this book and encouraging them to read through it may prompt them to complete the exercises, and perhaps seek further treatment if appropriate.

It's really important that you become aware of what's helpful and unhelpful when living with someone with a diagnosis of OCD, and some of that advice may be different to what you were expecting. As such, this book may help you make some positive changes in your own behaviour that could lead to the person with OCD making some positive decisions and changes about their situation.

→ What happens to me once I finish reading the book and completing the exercises?

Hopefully, if you read the book from start to finish you will have a clear idea of what OCD is, how it works, and how best to challenge and overcome your OCD. If you read this book and decide to seek further help, or if you want to talk to someone who understands your situation, then there are charities and organizations listed at the back of this book.

The majority of the charities involve those who have recovered from OCD and so fully understand what you are going through. They are able to offer free, impartial advice and many have a helpline that you can contact when you need some additional support. I would also encourage you to contact your GP and explain how you are feeling at the moment as they will be able to refer you for therapy. If you wish to seek private therapy, then I would recommend speaking to a few therapists to see who you have a connection with. Always ask about their qualifications and experiences in dealing with OCD and ask what the therapy process looks like, so that you have an idea of whether or not it is for you.

Also listed at the back of this workbook is a list of mental health organizations and they will be able to help you source qualified, accredited therapists who have the skills to help you.

2 What's Cognitive Behavioural Therapy (CBT)?

About this chapter

▶ This chapter will provide a brief overview of what Cognitive Behavioural Therapy (CBT) actually is. This is to provide an explanation of the therapy and to help you gain a better understanding of why CBT is an effective therapy for the treatment of OCD.

▶ (Please note this chapter is designed to give you a brief explanation of CBT, as opposed to an in-depth history of the development of the therapy.)

→ So what is Cognitive Behavioural Therapy (CBT)?

The name 'Cognitive Behavioural Therapy' (CBT) can be split into three main factors. First, we have our cognitions or 'thoughts'. These cognitions refer to how we think in different situations as well as our deeper cognitions. Our deeper cognitions are beliefs that we hold about ourselves, other people and the world around us. When we are considering our thoughts and our cognitions in relation to OCD, it is important to distinguish between our own thoughts e.g. what we think in a rational and logical moment, from our OCD thoughts e.g. what we think when we are highly anxious and viewing the world through an OCD filter.

For OCD we can consider two different trains of thought in CBT: one is your own thinking and one is your OCD thinking. In therapy we want to consider OCD as something separate from you from the word go. We see OCD as something you have *not* who you are (there will be more on this later in the book). As such it makes sense to consider the anxiety-provoking thoughts as belonging to OCD as opposed to them belonging to you.

The second part of CBT is the 'behavioural' element. This refers to our behaviours e.g. what we actually do in different situations. It is important to examine our behaviours as there are certain behaviours associated with OCD, which at first seem helpful in reducing our anxiety but which can in fact make the OCD worse, e.g. avoiding a situation or repeated checking behaviours.

The third part of CBT, the 'T' part, refers to the therapy. The therapy is where changes are made to both cognitions/thoughts and behaviours in order to achieve a different result in the same situation.

Often when we are anxious we believe that it is the situation that we need to change or avoid. For example, 'going on public transport makes me uncomfortable so I avoid using it' would be an example of changing the situation so you are not uncomfortable, e.g. not using public transport. However, in terms of treatment for OCD and anxiety, what we want to achieve is a level of comfort in all situations. While it is natural to have preferences in situations, what therapy aims to achieve is a feeling of control and empowerment in situations, instead of fear and anxiety. This means that you can make a decision based on personal preference, rather than OCD making those decisions for you. As such, if you decide that public transport no longer makes you uncomfortable but you still prefer driving yourself then that's fine.

However if OCD is telling you that something bad or embarrassing will happen on public transport and that's why you avoid it then that's not ok. The change that therapy wants to make is to put you back in the driving seat of your life. Therapy aims to equip you to take back control of your life and make decisions based on what you want, as opposed to what your OCD is telling you to do, and what your anxiety is least afraid of.

CBT is a very practical and experiential therapy, whereby you try new ways of doing or thinking and monitor the impact of making these changes. This is why a workbook is suited to the nature of CBT for OCD. This workbook will allow you to focus on situations, apply changes and monitor outcomes.

Therapy, whether using self-help resources, or engaging in face-to-face therapy, is a process of applying changes, doing things differently and discovering new ways of looking at, and being in, different situations. *It is not a passive process.*

Simply reading this book is not enough. You need to work through the exercises and take part in the activities and worksheets and apply some of the strategies. If you simply read this book but don't apply any of the strategies, then you will have a clear idea of what OCD is and how it works, but without taking these ideas and concepts on board and putting them into practice you are very unlikely to see change.

I know change is scary, but so is OCD. At least this way you are doing something about it. Many people want to get some help with a situation but struggle to see how things can be different and so the idea of change may be hard to imagine. This book will explain how these changes can be made, using a variety of strategies, and will give you an opportunity to try out these techniques in a way that is comfortable and doable for you.

CBT believes that many different aspects, including our thoughts and behaviours, interact with, and impact on, each other in different ways in different situations. Previous therapies such as **cognitive therapy** (Beck, 1976) and **behavioural therapy** (Wolpe, 1958) have focused solely on one area, such as thoughts or behaviours in isolation.

The section below describes how CBT develops these ideas further and forms a picture of a situation that incorporates both our thoughts and our behaviours and includes them in day-to-day situations.

→ CBT: taking theories further

CBT does not just focus on one area but instead it looks at the interactions between many different components. The premise of CBT is that our thoughts, feelings, behaviours and physical symptoms, together with the situation within which they occur, all affect and interact with each other. This is demonstrated in the 5-areas diagram below, which is often referred to as the 'hot cross bun' model (Padesky & Mooney, 1990) due to the appearance and 4 different segments.

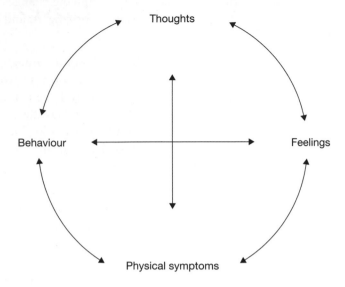

Situation

Thoughts

Behaviour

Feelings

Physical symptoms

As you can see from the diagram, CBT considers all these different elements to impact on each other. The benefit in using this view in therapy is that you can start with whatever approach feels most manageable and relevant for you. People may have very different 'starting points' in situations, with some focusing on physical symptoms and behaviours and others focusing on thoughts and feelings. By recognizing how all of these are interacting with and affecting each other in different situations, you are able to identify areas for change and then learn ways of implementing this change.

The 'hot cross bun' model is a really quick and easy way to formulate (e.g. plan out) any situation, and it can be useful to draw out different situations in this way to help you identify patterns.

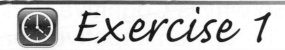

Exercise 1

Using the formulation diagram below, think of a situation (this doesn't necessarily need to be OCD related – this is just a practice exercise). Now draw out the situation considering how each of these areas was impacting on the others. An example has been given below to help you. Further copies can be found in the Appendix.

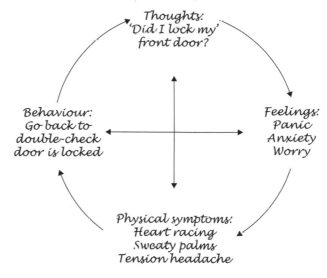

Situation: leaving the house

Thoughts:
'Did I lock my
front door?'

Feelings:
Panic
Anxiety
Worry

Physical symptoms:
Heart racing
Sweaty palms
Tension headache

Behaviour:
Go back to
double-check
door is locked

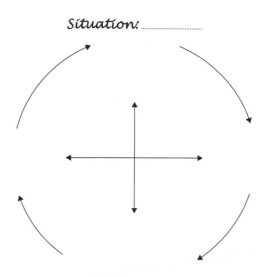

Situation: _____

→ So why is Cognitive Behavioural Therapy an effective treatment for Obsessive-Compulsive Disorder?

The reason why CBT is such an effective therapy for OCD is because it focuses on the thoughts, feelings and behaviours that may be maintaining the OCD, i.e. keeping it going. The next chapter looks in detail at what OCD is but, put briefly, OCD is a combination of thoughts and behaviours. The 'O' refers to the obsessions, which are intrusive thoughts, and the 'C' refers to compulsions, which are the OCD-related behaviours. By using a therapy that focuses on thoughts and behaviours to treat a disorder that is made up of thoughts and behaviours, you have a really good match for addressing and overcoming any OCD issues.

Key points to remember

▶ CBT focuses on our cognitions (thoughts), behaviours and on changing how these affect situations and maintain our OCD.

▶ CBT is a very practical and experiential therapy, whereby you try new ways of doing or thinking and monitor the impact of making these changes.

▶ You need to work through the exercises and take part in the activities and worksheets and apply some of the strategies, in order to see change.

▶ The reason why CBT is such an effective therapy for OCD is because it focuses on the thoughts, feelings and behaviours that may be maintaining the OCD.

▶ The CBT model is a good match for the model of OCD and thus makes a useful therapeutic approach.

Where to next?

 The next chapter looks at what OCD is (and isn't!) and discusses different types of OCD and OCD symptoms.

3 What's Obsessive-Compulsive Disorder (OCD)?

About this chapter

▶ This chapter focuses on OCD itself, looking at what OCD is and isn't, as well as considering OCD symptoms. There is a table to be completed that highlights different OCD symptoms and which will allow you to identify the problematic OCD symptoms that you are experiencing. There is also a description of recognized types of OCD, which you can consider and then work out those that apply to you and your situation.

→ Firstly, what isn't OCD?

Those of you familiar with my work will know that I always start a discussion about what OCD is by talking about what OCD isn't. I do this because there is a lot of confusion around OCD, and a great many inaccurate portrayals of OCD in the media have led to thousands of people thinking they have OCD when they don't. Thanks to recent TV shows, OCD seems to have become a 'fashionable' disorder with many people saying 'oh I'm a bit like that' when in fact there is nothing wrong with their mental health. These inaccurate portrayals are unhelpful as they can be seen to belittle those with genuine OCD and lead those without OCD to worry that they have a mental health problem.

So what isn't OCD? Many people will describe themselves as 'a bit OCD' if they like things done in a certain order or they like to keep their homes clean and tidy. This is not OCD. It is perfectly normal to have preferences for order and routine, and cleanliness works on a sliding scale with some people being very particular and other people being a lot more relaxed about their cleaning routines. So it is very possible to have an immaculate home, and have all your CDs alphabetized and all your books lined up in height order and not have OCD, despite what the media will tell you.

The difference between liking your surroundings to be neat and tidy and having OCD (which is rarely just about neatness, tidiness and cleanliness – but more on that later) is the level of *distress* felt by the individual. Those suffering from OCD will experience highly distressing thoughts and will develop rituals or 'compulsions' that they need to carry out. It will be extremely distressing for an individual if they cannot clear these thoughts or complete their ritual. So if you don't have OCD you may like things neat and tidy, and may experience some discomfort if things are messy, but you won't feel *distressed* by the situation.

However, someone with OCD cannot tolerate the level of distress that accompanies the situation and would have to act to resolve it. My patients with OCD will describe the *need* to complete their rituals saying 'even if someone put a gun to my head and told me to stop, I couldn't'.

OCD goes way beyond cleaning and has huge and devastating impacts on individuals' lives, which is why the media message of 'I'm a bit like that' is so unhelpful and misleading. There's no such thing as 'a bit' OCD.

→ So, what *is* OCD?

There are two main components to obsessive-compulsive disorder: 'obsessions' and 'compulsions'.

WHAT ARE OBSESSIONS?

Obsessions are recurrent and persistent thoughts, impulses or images that are intrusive, inappropriate and cause anxiety or distress. They pop into your mind and are not easily dismissed, meaning that even if you manage to distract yourself from the thoughts for a short while, they will return.

The thoughts, impulses or images are not simply excessive worries about real-life problems. For example, these won't be everyday worries about finances or illness that may be related to real-life events. Instead, these will be worries about things that may never happen or things that those without OCD would never think to worry about.

Often, the person having these obsessions will attempt to ignore or suppress such thoughts, impulses or images, or to neutralize them with some other thought or action (a compulsion). The person recognizes that the obsessional thoughts, impulses or images are a product of his or her own mind (not imposed from someone or something else). This is a big difference between OCD and other disorders. A person with OCD will, on some level, have insight into their problem and situation. Often, people will say to me 'I *know* this is crazy but I can't seem to stop doing it' or 'I *know* nothing bad will happen, I *know* this is just in my head … but I do these things just in case'. This is classic OCD thinking and the 'just in case' element is something that we will come on to later. Those with other disorders lack this insight into their own mental health and the impact of their thoughts and compulsions.

WHAT ARE COMPULSIONS?

Compulsions are repetitive behaviours (e.g. hand washing, ordering, checking) or mental acts (e.g. praying, counting, repeating words silently) that the person feels driven to perform in response to an obsession (intrusive thought), or according to rules that must be applied rigidly. People who carry out these compulsions or behaviours will often have a set way of doing things e.g. there will be a 'correct' way to wash or dress or drive to work and so on. If the compulsion is disturbed or interrupted then the person may feel they need to start again. This often means that people carry out their compulsions in secret, or develop ways of ensuring they can carry them out without other people knowing or being interrupted.

Sometimes the behaviours or mental acts are aimed at reducing distress or preventing some dreaded event or situation. However, these behaviours or mental acts may not be connected in a realistic way with what they are designed to neutralize or prevent, or could be clearly excessive.

For example, a mother may worry about accidentally poisoning her children and so may wash her hands repeatedly throughout the day whenever she touches anything, even if it is clean, for example, washing her hands in-between unloading items from the dishwasher.

As mentioned above, compulsions can be physical acts that people carry out or they can be thoughts, words or prayers that people say inside their heads. It may not always be obvious when someone is carrying out a compulsion.

→ Who has intrusive thoughts?

Everyone. Just take a second to read that again. Everyone has intrusive thoughts. We all have had an experience of driving along the motorway and having a thought about crashing the car. We've all held our new-born baby and have had intrusive thoughts about dropping them or harming them in some way. We have all experienced embarrassing, inappropriate, violent, sexual or distorted thoughts. Therefore those of you with OCD who think that there is something 'wrong' with you for having the thoughts that you have, need to start letting that idea go. You have exactly the same thoughts as someone without OCD. The only difference in this thinking is that *someone with OCD will give the thought a meaning*.

For example, if I'm holding my baby and I have a thought of throwing him down the stairs, without OCD I probably wouldn't register that thought, or if I did it would come and go very quickly (known as a 'fleeting thought'). However, if I had that same thought and I had OCD, I would immediately assume that that meant something about me as a person e.g. 'I'm a dangerous person', 'I'm going to harm my baby', 'I'm a terrible mother', 'I'm not safe to be around him anymore'. This may then lead to a great deal of angst and anxiety and possibly some avoidance or checking behaviours. So the thought itself is not different, rather it is the *meaning* that we apply to that thought that defines something as OCD or not. The meaning that is given to the thought is often quite alarming or shocking and that in itself can cause a lot of anxiety and worry, as well as the thoughts and worries that may follow.

→ How does OCD work?

OCD is a bully. Living with OCD is like living with a bully who never leaves your side. It stands over your shoulder making unhelpful comments about what you are doing or thinking and starts to put doubt in your mind about the simplest things that you have never questioned before.

You will just be minding your own business, trying to get on with your day, but this is made more difficult because you have OCD next to you saying 'have you done that right?'. 'Are you sure you turned that off?' 'Should you be thinking that?' 'What if this terrible thing happens and it's your fault?' 'Shouldn't you check that?'.

It is exhausting and belittling and mean. Those of us without OCD cannot begin to imagine what it must be like to live with this constant doubt and the way that this can build until you lose confidence and no longer feel able to trust yourself. However, OCD tricks us into thinking that it has a nicer side. It does this because when we feel extremely anxious or wound up OCD offers us a 'solution'. OCD will say 'I know you're scared – just go and check that and then you can relax'.

In this way, OCD offers us a way out of our anxiety, and it is easy to forget that it's anxiety we only have because OCD gave it to us in the first place! In this way OCD is similar to smoking cigarettes. Smoking seems to satisfy a craving for nicotine but that craving for nicotine only exists in the first place because you smoke – it's a vicious circle!

Of course when we begin to get OCD symptoms, we rarely stand back and think 'hmm I wonder if this is OCD' because OCD will start small and we may not even realize that we are thinking or doing anything out of the ordinary. Also, OCD fluctuates and can be exacerbated by anxiety and stress and so we may not notice the smaller OCD behaviours or checks until we experience something that makes us very anxious and then we may become a lot more aware of them.

→ I know these behaviours are bad for me, I know this is just OCD, so why am I still doing this years later?

The fluctuating nature and these 'helpful' suggestions that OCD offers explain why people get stuck in the cycle of OCD. People often want to know why they get stuck with OCD and this can be explained by some of the points below:

OCD IS NOT A CONSISTENT COMPANION

Much like living with a bully, if we lived with someone that only shouted at us or constantly called us names then we would leave. However, OCD fluctuates so just when you have had enough of OCD, you may have a good day or a couple of good weeks, where OCD seems to have taken a back seat. You start to enjoy life again and then bam! OCD strikes. This fluctuating nature means it isn't as straightforward as just getting fed up with OCD and stopping everything.

OCD PROVIDES COMFORT

The behaviours that result from the OCD do limit the anxiety for a short period of time. Therefore some OCD behaviours can appear helpful.

For example, if I'm worried about security and I check my front door is locked three times, that makes me feel better, and therefore checking my door seems a small price to pay for getting rid of the anxiety, so I continue to do it. The problem is OCD won't stop there. Once one thought or worry is eliminated then OCD will continue to offer up new doubts, worries and anxieties until we find a significant amount of time is being spent checking and worrying in an attempt to appease some of the OCD-driven anxieties.

At this point OCD becomes problematic. Instead of challenging the belief that you haven't locked your front door, you begin to doubt yourself more, and checking those three times becomes the habit. It is then very difficult to stop checking the door three times and return to not checking it at all. This then means if we are in a situation where we cannot check the door three times, we may become very anxious about this. Thoughts about our door may become intrusive and interrupt our day, and we may have a compulsion to go back and check the door again, or set aside more time to leave the house to accommodate this door checking. As you can see, what starts small can build and build until OCD is taking over your day.

OCD PICKS ON THE THINGS YOU LOVE AND THAT ARE IMPORTANT TO YOU

It is not a coincidence that OCD gives us intrusive thoughts about things or people that matter to us. This is a deliberate trick that OCD plays in order to gain as much attention as possible. After all, if OCD gave you loads of thoughts about someone you didn't know, or something of no significance to you, then it would be very easy to dismiss them as unimportant or irrelevant. OCD knows this and it doesn't like to be ignored. That's why it picks on our children, our friends, our loved ones and our families, and our own values. That's why it picks on our place of work, or our sense of safety and security. It deliberately picks things that it knows will grab our attention, and will be difficult to ignore.

This is yet another example of just how vile OCD truly is. OCD likes to be given lots of attention and needs constant anxiety and stress to thrive, which is why it picks on something that is so important to us, and which will be harder to dismiss quickly from our thoughts.

→ Do I have OCD?

You may be wondering whether you even have OCD. Below is a questionnaire that is often used to help people identify OCD symptoms (Foa et al. 2002). The purpose of including this questionnaire here isn't to provide you with a 'score' e.g. a number that will determine 'yes you have OCD' or 'no you don't'. However, completing the questionnaire will highlight any OCD symptoms you have, and to what extent they affect you.

Work your way through the questionnaire and tick any symptoms that apply to you, then rate how much that symptom distresses you.

Symptom	Do you have this thought? (✓)	How much does this thought distress you?(0 = not at all, 1 = a little, 2 = moderately, 3 = a lot, 4 = extremely)
Unpleasant thoughts come into my mind against my will and I cannot get rid of them		
I think contact with bodily secretions (perspiration, saliva, blood, urine, etc.) may contaminate my clothing or somehow harm me		
I ask people to repeat things to me several times, even though I understood the first time		
I wash and clean obsessively		
I mentally go over past events, conversations and actions to make sure that I didn't do or say something wrong		
I have collected so many things that they get in the way		
I check things more often than necessary		
I avoid using public toilets because I am afraid of disease or contamination		
I repeatedly check doors, windows, drawers, etc.		
I repeatedly check gas and water taps and light switches after turning them off		

I collect things I don't need		
I have thoughts of having hurt someone without knowing it		
I have thoughts that I might want to harm myself or others		
I get upset if objects are not arranged properly		
I feel obliged to follow a certain order when undressing, dressing or washing myself		
I feel compelled to count while I am doing things		
I am afraid of impulsively doing embarrassing of harmful things		
I need to pray to cancel bad thoughts or feelings		
I keep on checking forms or other things I have written		
I get upset at the sight of scissors, knives and other sharp objects in case I lose control with them		
I am excessively concerned about cleanliness		
I find it difficult to touch an object when I know it has been touched by strangers or by certain people		
I need things to be arranged in a particular order		

Further copies of this Exercise can be found in the Appendix.

As mentioned earlier, the purpose of including this table is not to provide you with an OCD 'score' that will determine your severity. However, you will be able to ascertain yourself how many of these OCD symptoms apply to you, and how much they are distressing you. This will give you an indicator as to the severity of your OCD. The more symptoms you recognized and were distressed by, the higher the level of OCD currently impacting on you. However many symptoms you recognized, this book will help you to learn strategies to overcome them.

Reader question:

Trichotillomania/compulsive skin picking

Although this book is not focusing specifically on trichotillomania (hair-pulling disorder) or excoriation (skin-picking disorder), I did receive an email asking for a brief explanation of what these disorders are and how best to approach overcoming them.

Those who have trichotillomania suffer from compulsive urges to pull out their own hair. Sufferers most commonly pull hair from their scalp, eyelashes or eyebrows. Those with this disorder often have bald spots where they have pulled out a lot of hair from the same spot. This can lead to some anxiety and embarrassment around appearance, leading people to cover up using hats, scarves or wigs, or draw on eyebrows and use false eyelashes.

The symptoms of trichotillomania, alongside the hair pulling itself, may include: a) feeling tense before pulling hair or when trying to resist the urge to pull hair; b) feeling relieved, satisfied, or pleased after acting on the impulse to pull hair; c) distress or problems at work or in social life due to hair pulling.

The reason why trichotillomania becomes problematic, beside the social and emotional impact, is that if left untreated those who pull their hair are at higher risk of infection, skin damage and permanent hair loss. There are also common psychological effects to hair-pulling such as depression, social isolation (usually due to embarrassment), body image issues and low self-esteem.

Excoriation (skin-picking disorder) has only been recently identified and named as a disorder in the DSM 5 (Diagnostic and Statistical Manual – version 5), although it is estimated that between 2 and 4 per cent of the population could be diagnosed with this disorder. While many of us may absentmindedly pick or scratch at our skin, excoriation is characterized by constant and recurrent picking at your skin, resulting in skin lesions. It is very common for those who pick at their skin in this way to suffer significant distress and/or impairment in social, occupational or other important areas of functioning. If left untreated then the resulting problems may include medical issues such as infections, skin lesions, scarring and physical disfigurement.

The best treatment approach for both of these conditions is to start by identifying the triggers that cause someone to pull their hair out or pick at their skin. These may be external situation triggers or internal emotional triggers. Once these have been identified, then the habit of hair-pulling or skin-picking can be replaced by something else, e.g. holding something in the hand that would normally be doing the picking/pulling. Alongside this work, a therapist can also help you to address any unhelpful thinking that contributes to the urge to skin-pick/pull your hair.

It is also a good idea to learn some relaxation and stress-management techniques as stress can be a trigger in these situations. These treatment options combined can help firstly reduce, and then later eliminate altogether, the urge to pull one's hair/pick skin.

For those seeking medication alongside treatment, some find an antidepressant known as a selective serotonin re-uptake inhibitor (SSRI) to be useful in helping to curb very intense urges. However, research indicates that medication works best when used alongside a therapy, as opposed to being used in isolation.

→ Different types of OCD

Listed below are some of the different types of OCD. You may feel you can relate to one or more of these categories or 'subtypes' of OCD.

CONTAMINATION

Those affected by this type of OCD will experience feelings of discomfort associated with contamination and may wash or clean excessively to reduce these feelings of distress. For example, you might feel that your hands are dirty or contaminated after touching a door handle or worry that you will contaminate others with your germs. To get rid of these feelings, you might wash your hands repeatedly. Within this category sits the 'mental contamination' category.

Mental contamination refers to a similar feeling of dirt or contamination but without the physical contact. In other words, sometimes we can be made to *feel* dirty even though we haven't touched something. This may be due to thinking or seeing something distasteful, someone we dislike, or thinking something inappropriate. When experiencing mental contamination, we may attempt to deal with it in the same way as physical contamination by excessively washing or showering until we feel clean again.

RUMINATIONS

Rumination refers to the way we may focus on and think about something over and over again even if we are no longer in that particular situation. It's often used to try to help us 'analyse' our thoughts or work through something that has happened. When we are ruminating it can feel as though our mind is 'stuck' on a certain point and cannot move forward.

People experiencing rumination often have intense thoughts relating to possible harm to themselves or others and use checking rituals to relieve their distress. For example, we might imagine our house burning down and then continually drive by our house to make sure that there is no fire. In addition, we may feel that by simply thinking about a disastrous event, we are increasing the likelihood of such an event actually happening.

'PURE O' (OBSESSIONS WITHOUT VISIBLE COMPULSIONS OR SO-CALLED 'PURE OBSESSIONS')

This symptom subtype often relates to unwanted obsessions surrounding sexual, religious or aggressive themes. For example, we could experience intrusive thoughts about being a rapist or a paedophile or that we will attack someone. This is called 'Pure O', as often people describe themselves as not carrying out compulsions when they have these thoughts. However, we may often use mental rituals such as reciting particular words, counting or praying to relieve the anxiety we experience when we have these involuntary thoughts. Triggers related to obsessions are usually avoided at all costs.

'JUST RIGHT' – SYMMETRY OBSESSIONS WITH ORDERING, ARRANGING AND COUNTING COMPULSIONS

We may feel a strong need to arrange and rearrange objects until they are 'just right'. For example, we might feel the need to constantly arrange our shirts so that they are ordered precisely by colour. This symptom subtype can also involve thinking or saying sentences or words over and over again until the task is accomplished perfectly. There is often no quantifiable number as to how many times these rituals should be completed, instead we carry them out until things feel 'just right'.

HOARDING

Hoarding used to be considered part of OCD and by some professionals is still included under this category, although new classification shows hoarding to be considered as related to but separate from OCD. Hoarding involves the collection of items that are judged to be of limited value by others, such as old magazines, clothes, receipts, junk mail, notes or containers.

When hoarding it is common for living space to become so cluttered that it becomes impossible to live in. Hoarding is often accompanied by obsessional fears of losing items or possessions that may be needed one day and excessive emotional attachment to objects. Those hoarding are likely to experience high anxiety and depression and often encounter huge interference with day-to-day living. NB: compulsive hoarding can occur independently of OCD.

It doesn't really matter which of these categories you feel you belong to (if any) as the strategies outlined in this book will help you to challenge the thoughts and behaviours associated with all types of OCD, and so treatment will be effective regardless of category. However sometimes these categories can be useful for summarizing for ourselves or for others what the experience of OCD is like and why it affects us the way it does.

Reader question:

Is OCD 'contagious' – will I give this to my children?

The idea of passing on OCD to our children is naturally very distressing and this is a question my colleagues and I are asked a lot in clinic. While there is no evidence of an 'OCD gene' at present, what we do know is that it is possible for children to pick up on OCD behaviours and begin to mimic them at a young age.

'I never really thought about what I was doing around the kids. After all, in my mind everything I was doing was to keep them safe, so I almost didn't register that they'd be watching me do all these things. For me the crunch point came when I arrived home one day to find my little girl tying plastic bags to her brother's feet. "Don't walk on the carpet!" she screamed at him, "Mummy has hoovered and she will get really upset with you!"

My jaw hit the floor. Is this what my kids think of me? I knew then that I had to change. My daughter was only five at the time. You want your children to grow up respecting and admiring you – not doing loads of weird things that they've learned from you! It was a wake-up call for me. I knew I had to change.'

As you can see, it is possible for children to pick up on behaviours and attitudes around the house far more easily than we might think/be aware of.

Something that I notice a lot when I talk to parents and children with OCD is that often 'anxiety' becomes something to be extremely feared and avoided in the household. This often leaves children feeling responsible for keeping their parents calm and anxiety-free and this inflated responsibility can cause huge problems for children. Listen to Anthony's account below.

Case study: Anthony

'Growing up I knew my dad was a bit different to other dads. He'd be at the school gates half an hour early and be pacing outside. It became embarrassing – people would start pointing and saying "Look Anthony, your dad is here", "What is he doing here?", etc. It was really awkward. I was never allowed to go to a friend's house after school as my dad just couldn't tolerate the anxiety of not knowing where I was. He'd have thoughts that I would be taken ill and he wouldn't be there to help me and I'd die.

It started for Dad because when I was younger I swallowed a battery and started choking. I was fine but Dad walked into the room and found me choking and he had to help clear my throat. I wasn't that bothered after that but Dad started to pick things up and everything smaller than his hand went on to a top shelf. My mum told him repeatedly that I was fine but it didn't matter. As I grew up Dad became worse and worse and eventually as a teenager I just went along with it. Yeah I wanted to go and hang out with my friends but I couldn't bear to see Dad get so worked up. He'd always come and find me and ruin whatever I was doing, and it was just embarrassing and spoilt things. I got really anxious if I was late home as I knew Dad would be in a right state.

I'm off to uni next year and I haven't told Dad where I'm applying. I can't bear the thought of him coming to visit me to check I'm ok. I can't have him ruin uni as well … I just can't.'

You can see from Anthony's story that although he didn't develop any OCD behaviours himself, he did learn to accommodate his dad's OCD and went along with whatever his dad needed him to do in order to make his dad feel better.

As you can imagine, this had a huge impact on Anthony's relationship with his father when he was older, and he relished the freedom of the prospect of university. Anthony felt he had missed out on so much because of his dad's OCD. He said he didn't resent it as he loved his father but it made him sad and he found socializing awkward, since he hadn't been able to socialize much during his early years. Anthony worries about becoming a father himself now as he worries he will become like his dad.

So although OCD isn't necessarily genetically passed on, the impacts can be far-reaching and result in family members and children developing high levels of anxiety and their own OCD-related behaviours in order to accommodate your condition. Often, watching our children develop these behaviours provides a great deal of motivation to get better and get rid of OCD for the whole family, not just ourselves.

Key points to remember

▶ There are two main components to obsessive-compulsive disorder, which are 'obsessions' and 'compulsions'.

▶ Obsessions are recurrent and persistent thoughts, impulses, or images that are intrusive, inappropriate and cause anxiety or distress.

▶ Compulsions are repetitive behaviours (e.g., hand washing, ordering, checking) or mental acts (e.g., praying, counting, repeating words silently) that the person feels driven to perform in response to an obsession (intrusive thought), or according to rules that must be applied rigidly.

▶ OCD is a bully.

▶ You are bigger and stronger than OCD. Yes it is a bully, but it's a bully that can be defeated.

Where to next?

Now that you have a clear understanding of what OCD is, the next chapter is talking you through preparing for therapy, so that you can begin to make positive changes, and reduce the impact of OCD.

4 Preparing for therapy

About this chapter

▶ Before embarking on therapy, it is important to prepare yourself, overcome any misgivings, have a clear idea of what it is that you will be doing, and decide whether this is the right time for you. Preparation is an important part of undertaking therapy and this chapter is designed to help you prepare for working through this book, and therefore get the most out of it.

▶ As part of this preparation we look at why we need to set goals for therapy, and guide you as to how to set your own goals. By the end of this chapter you will have established and recorded your own goals for overcoming OCD.

→ Why now?

Whenever someone wants to start therapy one of the questions that the therapist is always interested in is 'why now?'. If you have struggled with a particular diagnosis, such as OCD, for many years, why does now feel like the best time to start overcoming this?

⏰ *Exercise 3*

Take a moment to think about what has led you to purchase this book and why now feels as though it is the right time for you to start overcoming your OCD.

List these reasons below:

_____

_____

_____

_____

_____

_____

_____

_____

_____

_____

_____

_____

_____

_____

_____

Take some time to review your reasons above. Now ask yourself the following questions and consider if any of your reasons for starting therapy are due to the reasons listed below:

– Is anyone forcing you to do this?

_____

_____

_____

_____

_____

– Has anyone threatened consequences if you don't address this e.g. the end of a relationship?

_____

_____

_____

_____

_____

– Do you feel under pressure to tackle your OCD even though you may not feel ready?

_____

_____

_____

_____

_____

_____

If you have answered 'yes' to the above questions and if your reasons listed above feel related to these or other externally driven reasons, then it may be that you are not ready for therapy.

Wanting to engage in therapy solely to appease someone else is almost never successful. Completing therapy and facing the challenges involved in it can be tough, and if you are solely doing this for someone else, then it is unlikely that you will be able or willing to push yourself out of your comfort zone and tackle these issues. While it may be that you have someone in your life who is desperate for things to change for you and for them, it is important that you are motivated to start challenging your OCD for your own reasons.

Look at the list below and see if any of these apply to you:

▶ I didn't know this was OCD but now I do I want to do something about it

▶ I always thought my OCD was untreatable but would like things to be different

▶ I am fed up of living like this and want something to change

▶ I want to make changes but I'm not sure how

▶ I used to be able to do so much more – I want to get back to the 'old' me

▶ I can't wait to kick OCD out of my life – it's long overdue and I am looking forward to a life that is OCD-free.

If the above statements sound like you, or match your reasons for wanting to engage in treatment for overcoming your OCD, then you are much more likely to have successful therapy.

You need to be ready and willing to make changes, and you need to want things to be different in your life in order to fully engage with the treatment for OCD.

→ Do you accept this is OCD?

While it is perfectly possible (and normal) to have some doubts and fears around whether this is OCD or whether there is something more deeply 'wrong' with you, on some level you need to have an understanding that this is OCD. For example, if you believe that your thoughts are not OCD but are instead being given to you from an external source e.g. a higher power, or a malevolent force, then it is possible that you are struggling with difficulties outside OCD, and it would be good to discuss these with your GP or a mental health professional. Those with OCD have some insight into their thoughts (obsessions) and actions (compulsions) and are able to identify that these are out of character.

As you can see from John's account, knowing that this was OCD was not enough to stop him acting on and responding to his intrusions. However, John did have good insight into the fact that he couldn't actually control the roads and that this was OCD thinking. This level of insight is what distinguishes OCD from other disorders and so it is important that you are able to see OCD for what it is, even if you doubt yourself from time to time.

→ Can you be honest with yourself?

Many of our OCD thoughts (obsessions) concern themes and ideas that distress us and we need to be able to face up to OCD and what we are thinking, even if it is distressing. For example, some very common obsessions and themes concern:

▶ Thoughts of hurting others

▶ Thoughts of a violent nature

▶ Thoughts of a sexual nature

▶ Thoughts that feel inappropriate or abhorrent in some way

▶ Thoughts that we feel ashamed of/wouldn't admit to publicly.

One of the great things about working through a book like this is that you are able to address these obsessions privately, which will alleviate some of the anxiety that comes with having to talk to someone face to face. However, you need to be able to admit to yourself and address the obsessions you're having.

It is likely that you spend a great deal of time trying not to have these thoughts, and that is perfectly normal and a common part of having OCD. You are going to need to be honest with yourself and be able to face the uglier side of OCD in order to overcome it. If you find it unbearable to even think of acknowledging and addressing these obsessions, then it will become difficult to apply the techniques and complete the exercises within this book. However, there are lots of reasons why people resist acknowledging their obsessions, so I would encourage you to keep reading as there will be exercises that will allow you to overcome this and then begin the work from there.

→ Let's face the fears

There are many very common fears that can prevent people from starting treatment for OCD. Listed below are some of the most common fears. Have a read through these and see which, if any, apply to you. If some of these fears match your own, then try working through the exercises to start overcoming them.

COMMON FEAR 1

I read somewhere/heard on the radio/my GP told me that OCD is untreatable and I worry that I am only setting myself up for failure.

Before OCD was better understood, it is true that clinicians struggled to understand what was going on for individuals with OCD, and therefore they struggled to offer a successful treatment. Nowadays, since OCD is classified as an anxiety disorder, many therapists who regularly treat anxiety, but who have no experience of dealing with OCD, will try and fail to successfully treat OCD. The problem is that without understanding OCD and the way it works treatment can very quickly fall into a 'tug of war' with a therapist saying 'just stop doing what you're doing' and the person with OCD saying 'but I can't!'. These two factors combined have led to a belief that OCD is untreatable. However this is not the case. Once you have a good understanding of OCD, how it affects you and how to get rid of it, there is absolutely no reason to think that your OCD is untreatable.

COMMON FEAR 2

I've had this for years and years – surely this makes it harder to treat?

Due to the length of time it takes people to understand what is wrong and get a diagnosis of OCD, it is very rare to treat someone that hasn't had OCD for many years. In fact in my entire career I have only ever worked with two people who had OCD for less than a year, and I have met a LOT of people with OCD. The length of time doesn't make a difference – the treatment is the same whether you've had OCD for 2 years or 20. It's important not to view your OCD as untreatable, as holding this belief will only serve to demotivate you and put you off trying to overcome it.

Challenge that thought: When you next have the thought 'My OCD is definitely untreatable' challenge it and try thinking 'My OCD might be very treatable – I certainly won't know unless I try!'. This gentle challenging of the thought will open your mind to the possibility that perhaps you can overcome this and will make starting therapy feel more hopeful.

COMMON FEAR 3

I've had this for so long I've forgotten how to be 'me'. I don't know who I am without OCD.

This is a very common fear for those affected by OCD. Often it can feel as though your whole life has been overtaken by OCD and it's hard to imagine functioning without it. How do you go back to old roles e.g. spouse/partner, friend, parent, colleague, etc. as someone who is completely well and no longer battling with OCD? What do you do with your time if you are not constantly obsessing or carrying out compulsions? Who are you without OCD?

 *Exercise 4*

It is important to try to figure out who you are without OCD, and be able to picture your life OCD-free, in order to motivate you throughout treatment. Try some of the exercises below to help you uncover the 'real' you that has been buried under the OCD.

Who did you used to be? Think back to a time before OCD/when OCD was less prominent in your life. What were you doing? What did you enjoy? Who were you friends with? Take some time to think about this and write a list below:

Who I used to be:

_____

_____

_____

_____

_____

_____

_____

_____

_____

_____

_____

_____

_____

_____

_____

_____

I can't remember a time without OCD. If you cannot think back to a time when you weren't battling OCD then look at the list of words below and ask yourself which ones you would like to have in your future, without OCD:

Fun	Sociable	Enjoyable	Chatty	Happy
Working	Confident	Independent	Free	Caring
	Spontaneous	Carefree	Motivated	

The above words represent elements that are often difficult to have in our lives when we have OCD. If you've circled some (or all!) of the above then hold them in mind. Even if you're not sure how to achieve these yet, it's good to have an image in mind of what you look like without OCD.

⏱ Exercise 5

Think of someone you admire.

If you still struggle to know what you want life to be like when you are free from OCD, then think of someone you know or admire and write down a list of their characteristics, and what it is you admire about them. Are these characteristics that you would like for yourself? Make a list of the people and their characteristics below and highlight the ones you would like for yourself:

Person I admire	What I like about them	Which of their characteristics would I like to have?
e.g. Jessica Ennis-Hill	Strong, confident, determined, athletic, nice smile, seems happy, genuine, open, talks about how things really are, not fake	I would like to be confident and open about my struggles in the way Jessica is. I'd like her determination and to be genuinely happy

Having identified the characteristics that you like in others helps you to paint a picture of what is important to you, and how you would like to be without OCD. Again this can serve as a good reminder and motivator throughout therapy of what you are striving for and why.

Those whom I have worked with will know that I am a big fan of time travelling. It is one of my favourite techniques to try and it works like this: if you want to achieve something, go forward in your mind to a time where you have achieved it and ask yourself how you got there. Ask yourself what small change you had to make today in order to bring you closer to your goal of being where you are. It sounds a slightly odd concept, but 'time travelling' actually helps us to think of what we need to do in a very practical sense to make changes. This can work for many different goals/ambitions and so you can try it whenever you have anything you want to achieve.

In this context time travel to a time when you are OCD free and ask yourself:

▶ What are you doing now?

▶ How did you get there?

▶ What did you need to change?

Try a bit of time travelling and enjoy the ride!

COMMON FEAR 4

The idea of treatment itself scares me.

If you have had previous treatment, or heard a lot about treatment, then you may have developed ideas or views around it and be scared by what it entails. I'm not going to deny that treatment can feel a bit scary. This is partly because people have a lot of emotion invested in their treatment, and so the fear of treatment failure can be scary. Also, treatment can be scary because it involves challenging some ideas and behaviours that have become intricately woven into your everyday life.

Therefore in treatment when we ask you to 'take a risk' by stopping a behaviour or trying something new, there is no doubt that this is challenging. However, we need to remember that the 'risks' you are taking are the same risks everyone takes several times in their day-to-day life without harmful consequences. Also remember that your therapist (in this case, me, writing this book) is never going to ask you to do something that a) they wouldn't do themselves or b) that they believe could cause any harm.

→ Let's weigh it up

When treatment feels scary and this is putting people off attempting it, I ask them to complete a cost-benefit analysis. This is looking at some of the concerns you had about starting treatment, some of the possible gains of undergoing treatment and thinking about the impact of these on your life.

Exercise 6

The table below looks at the areas of our lives that OCD can affect and then there is a column for the 'costs' of the OCD and another for the 'benefits' of overcoming it. Complete the table with your own experiences; an example has been included to get you started:

Area of life affected by OCD	The cost of the OCD	The benefit of overcoming it
Work: Productivity Quality Concentration Promotion Financial situation Relationship with colleagues/boss	e.g. too anxious to concentrate at work. Constantly worried about making mistakes.	I'd be able to forget about work when I got home. Better relationship with my boss. I could finally ask for that promotion.

Personal relationships:
Partner and effect on
relationship
Time with friends
Ability to socialize
Level of honesty
Closeness to others

Parenting (if applicable):
Quality time with children
Enjoy being a parent
Be fully 'present' with my
children
Able to be emotionally
available for my children
Able to be a good role model
Able to teach them about
managing stress and
anxiety
Not involving them in my
OCD rituals, etc.

Being me:

Able to do whatever I want
Able to progress as a person
Able to learn new things
Travel
Grow in confidence
Be engaged in the world
around me

Other key areas (specify):

Take some time to review the cost-benefit analysis you have completed above. Do the benefits of overcoming OCD outweigh the costs of living with it? If the answer is 'no', then it is possible that now is not the right time to engage in treatment and make changes, and you may want to wait and re-evaluate at a time when you feel more motivated to make some changes and be free of OCD. If the answer is 'yes', then now is as good a time as any to treat OCD – let's get started!

→ Setting your therapy goals

WHY DO I NEED TO SET GOALS?

A key part of Cognitive Behavioural Therapy (CBT) is to collaboratively set goals with an individual prior to starting therapy. Setting goals has many purposes such as:

1 *Guiding the therapy*. Like any journey, by knowing where you want to go to you are better able to plan your route. The same applies to therapy. By knowing where you want to be at the end of your therapeutic journey, you are better able to understand what you need to do in order to get there. We've already started to look at who you want to be post-therapy. Setting goals allows you to 'draw the map' for your therapy so that you can clearly see where you are going, and what you are heading towards.

2 *Monitoring progress*. Often we spend so long focusing on where we are going that we forget to look back and see how far we have come. The same is true in therapy and this is where goals are so helpful. By having tangible aims and goals for therapy you are better able to monitor your progress and realize when you have achieved something.

This is particularly important when you become frustrated or disheartened – the goals become a reality check so that when you feel 'I haven't achieved anything' you have proof to the contrary and can look back and say 'actually, I've achieved loads!'.

3 *Keeping on track*. Having specific goals and aims acts as a motivator for continuing through therapy. As long as your goals are meaningful to you, and you really want to achieve them, they can be really helpful for motivating you and pushing you through challenges.

As you can see, setting goals is a really important and useful element of therapy. However, we also want to make sure that we are setting the right goals. In particular with OCD, we want to make sure that it is you that is setting your goals and not your OCD. Within CBT we use the SMART method of goal-setting (Doran, 1981). This method is outlined below.

Read through the explanation and then we start setting your own therapy goals.

→ So what do we mean by SMART goals?

SMART goals refer to goals that are Specific, Measurable, Attainable, Realistic and Time-limited. Read on for further explanation.

SPECIFIC

When we set a goal we need to be very clear about what we mean. For example, when starting therapy people often tell me 'I just want to be happier' or 'I want to worry less' or 'I want to feel less anxious'. While all of these make sense, they are not SMART goals as they are not specific. Therefore when you are setting goals, think about what you actually mean. For example; if your goal is to be happier then think about what being happier would look like for you. What would you be doing if you were happier that you are not doing at the moment? If someone walked past you in the street, how would they know you were feeling happier? How would you look different if you were happier? What would change for you if you were happier? By asking these questions we may uncover the following goals:

If I were happier I'd be more sociable and bubbly. I'd make more effort with my appearance and I would speak to more people. Therefore my goals are to make new friends and try new activities where I'll meet people. I also want to make more of myself and my appearance. I will make sure I wear decent clothes and do my hair every day and I will invite my colleagues for a drink at the end of the week.

These goals as outlined here become specific.

MEASURABLE

We need to be able to measure our progress and so the goals we set ourselves are much more successful if they are measurable. For example, it is much better to set a goal of 'I want to be able to check everything in the kitchen is switched off just once' rather than 'I want to stop checking'. The goal 'I want to be able to check everything in the kitchen is switched off just once' is easily measured as one can simply record the number of times we check everything in the kitchen.

Try to think of a way you can measure your goal and make that part of it.

ATTAINABLE

Our goals should be realistic and achievable. For example, if you were planning on losing weight, you wouldn't set the goal 'I'd like to lose 4 stone this week' as that is physically impossible and so you could never achieve this goal.

Sometimes with OCD it is hard to imagine what feels attainable and achievable, so set yourself smaller goals if this helps, even if they are day by day or hour by hour. It doesn't matter how small the step is, as long as it is in the right direction. For example, a daily goal may be 'today I won't text my partner to see if he got to work safely'. That's not promising that you won't ever text your partner to check their wellbeing ever again, but it's setting a goal that may feel attainable for one day only.

Try it to see what you come up with.

REALISTIC

Keeping our goals realistic means they are more applicable to our day-to-day life. Having a goal of 'I want to stop worrying' is unrealistic. Everybody experiences periods of anxiety, and life events which lead them to worry, and it is unrealistic to think that we will never worry ever again. However, a realistic goal may be 'I would like to have a 'typical' reaction to events and then be able to let them go by the end of the day, rather than play them over and over in my mind and constantly worry about them'. This is a much more realistic goal that instantly makes it 'doable'.

Unrealistic goals, as lovely as they sound, will always remain a fantasy.

TIME-LIMITED

The purpose of having a time limit on a goal is to keep momentum going. The time limit serves as a deadline and we can share this with others so that they can help and support us to achieve our goal by the deadline. Again it is important to keep the deadline realistic within this time limit, so consider a realistic time frame and set your goal accordingly.

Within therapy you revisit and review your goals constantly in order to see what is left to achieve, and set new goals for the future. This helps to keep therapy active in our day-to-day life and means that we continue to make progress. Therefore don't worry too much if you are unsure whether a goal is going to work for you. Set some goals and then come back to review them in a few weeks and see if they are working for you.

→ Set your therapy goals

Exercise 7

Use the space below to consider your own goals for overcoming OCD.

_____

_____

_____

_____

_____

_____

_____

_____

_____

_____

_____

_____

_____

_____

_____

Now reconsider the goals and use the table below to check if they follow SMART principles:

Goal	Specific ✓	Measurable ✓	Attainable ✓	Realistic ✓	Time-limited ✓
e.g. write your goal here and then review it across the columns – does it meet the criteria?					

Once you have reviewed your goals and you are happy with them, make a copy of them and keep them somewhere visible. This helps keep your goals, and therefore your motivation, in mind and also encourages you to do something to work towards these goals every day.

A further copy of this Exercise can be found in the Appendix.

Key points to remember

▶ Before embarking on therapy, it is important to prepare yourself, overcome any misgivings, have a clear idea of what it is that you will be doing, and decide whether this is the right time for you.

▶ You need to be ready and willing to make changes, and you need to want things to be different in your life in order to fully engage with the treatment for OCD.

▶ You need to be able to accept that what you are experiencing is OCD.

▶ It is important to have a clear picture of what you are trying to achieve in order to motivate you and encourage you through the process of therapy.

▶ Make sure you set SMART goals to give you the best chance of success.

Where to next?

The next chapter focuses on building your 'formulation'. Your formulation describes how your OCD started and what may be maintaining it today. The chapter will show you how to build your own formulation, giving you examples to help you.

5 Painting the picture of your OCD – creating your formulation

▶ A key part of Cognitive Behavioural Therapy is the development of the formulation. A formulation is a way of drawing out your experiences of OCD and can help you to understand what has led to you developing OCD and what keeps the OCD going or 'maintains' the OCD.

▶ This chapter is designed to show you how to draw out your own formulation, in order to gain a better understanding of your own OCD. You will be talked through the different stages that make up your formulation, and shown how to complete these to build the picture of your OCD. You will be given examples following a case study throughout in order to help make this process clearer and easier.

→ Why do I need to know where my OCD came from?

You may feel that knowing that you have OCD is enough for you and that you don't need to take time out to understand how and when it developed. However, a formulation serves multiple purposes in therapy and so it is a useful tool to develop as part of your own journey in overcoming OCD.

By understanding and drawing links between the beginnings of your OCD with how it affects you today, you are able to gain a deeper understanding of the issues that may be keeping your OCD active or 'present' with you today. Once you understand these then you are able to challenge and overcome them and, in doing so, you can remove some of the thoughts or beliefs that leave you vulnerable to OCD.

The idea of a formulation is that it is an active and organic element to therapy, which shifts and changes as you make progress. Therefore it can be handy to keep your formulation in your therapy notebook/ folder, or draw it in this workbook. This will allow you to return to it throughout therapy and be able to review and update it as you make progress. It can be helpful to keep a copy of your original formulation as this can be a good source of reference, and allows you to recognize how far you have come when progress feels a bit slow.

→ Getting started

When completing your formulation in therapy, we look at different parts of the formulation and then we piece it all together to build a picture of how your OCD developed. The starting point for any formulation is to look at your 'early experiences'.

EARLY EXPERIENCES

When we look at your early experiences, we are looking at situations and events that occurred when you were younger, which may have made you vulnerable to developing OCD. There are many different experiences that can contribute to the development of OCD and they may not be immediately apparent, or obviously connected to OCD, so it is important to give yourself plenty of time and head space to think these ideas through.

It can also be helpful to discuss the formulation with those who know you well if you are comfortable to do so, as they may be able to help you piece your formulation together. Some people find it helpful to complete several formulations in order to help them to understand different elements of their OCD, and as such they may complete more than one formulation in therapy. This is absolutely fine and you can complete the formulation as many times as you need to, in order to make sense of your situation.

To start with your early experiences, you need to think about what may have started or contributed towards the development of your OCD. It can be helpful to think about some of the attitudes those around you had towards anxiety and other emotions, and also elements such as parenting style, religion and beliefs held in the family, etc.

Read through the example case study below to give you ideas for your own formulation.

Case study: Adam

Adam is a 24-year-old who was diagnosed with OCD four years ago. Adam describes himself as 'a bit of a worrier' and finds that he is anxious about making mistakes at work, which leads him to continually check documents and emails before sending them. When working on Adam's formulation, we discussed his early experiences and this is how he described them:

My parents always told me that education was important and my older brother was really bright and everything seemed really easy for him. My homework would always take me twice as long as his took him. I'm not stupid but he did things so quickly – it just wasn't normal! I used to pretend that I'd finished mine at the same time and then I'd take it up to my room and finish it there. I'd spend so many extra hours on my homework. I couldn't ever tell anyone because I thought they'd think I was stupid. My parents didn't really put pressure on me directly but they'd always talk to friends about 'our clever boys'. I felt like a fraud. I didn't know how to tell them that I was struggling. I just kept working harder and harder.

My grades were good but I didn't do anything except work. Even going away for a weekend stressed me out when I was younger because I didn't know how I'd get my work done. No one ever talked about feelings or stress in my family so I never told anyone. My parents were really rude about people who they thought of as 'lazy' and would often make comments about people they worked with who weren't 'pulling their weight'. I was scared to tell them I was struggling in case they thought I was lazy and just told me to work harder. This went on until I left home and came to uni.

As you can see, when discussing his early experiences, Adam raised a number of issues which included:

1 Being told and believing that education is important

2 A brother who he perceived as 'brighter' and more academically able than himself

3 An inability to tell anyone he was struggling

4 Secretive behaviour as a coping strategy

5 Negative family attitude towards 'laziness'

6 Long-term behaviour (from childhood until leaving home).

As you can see, Adam was able to identify some key early experiences that he felt had contributed towards his OCD.

NB: It's not a blame game! When discussing early experiences, people often become uncomfortable that they might be seen as trying to 'blame' someone or something for the development of their OCD. This is not the case. When formulating, we are not looking for a scapegoat. Instead we are looking at early experiences to see what may have made us vulnerable to developing OCD in the first place.

Therefore don't feel guilty – you're not being asked to identify someone to pin this on! Instead, just take some time to honestly consider the early experiences that you feel may have played a part in developing your OCD. It is quite possible that someone may make a casual passing comment that leads to the development of OCD. This doesn't mean that we blame them as it was never their intention to cause us problems and so this is not a process of blame, rather it is uncovering and naming what has happened.

Exercise 8

Take some time to consider your own early experiences. Write them out in full below and then summarize them into bullet points, as we did with Adam in the above example. Write these in the space below:

_____

_____

_____

_____

_____

_____

_____

_____

_____

_____

_____

_____

_____

_____

_____

_____

_____

Summary points of early experiences:

1 _____

_____

2 _____

_____

3 _____

_____

4 _____

_____

5 _____

_____

6 _____

_____

CRITICAL INCIDENT

The critical incident in a formulation refers to an incident or event that you believe has triggered your current episode of OCD. This may relate to a specific life event, such as leaving home, having a baby, getting married, changing jobs, losing a loved one, or moving house. Or it may just be an ordinary day at work/school/home that triggered your OCD.

NB: this is different to the early experiences section of the formulation. The early experiences section looks at the experiences that may have left you vulnerable to developing OCD. The critical incident part of the formulation refers to a specific event or situation that you believe triggered your OCD.

Let's go back to Adam's formulation for an example.

Case study: Adam

My critical incident was definitely leaving home and going to university. I think coming to uni just felt like way too much pressure. Suddenly I was completely responsible for myself, my wellbeing and my progress. It was so different to school. I didn't know anyone and I'd moved quite far away so didn't have any friends or family nearby. It was a really pressurized time. Everyone else was going out and having fun in the run up to our first course assignment whereas I stayed in studying for ages. People thought I was a real geek and didn't really invite me to socialize with them. I think they thought it was odd that I was so worked up about one small assignment that wasn't even being assessed. Leaving home was definitely when the checking started – I'd say that was the point at which I developed full-blown OCD.

As you can see from the above, Adam's critical incident is clearly defined in his mind as when he left home.

Take some time to think about what you believe your critical incident to be.

▶ What was it that caused the OCD to start?

_____

_____

_____

_____

▶ What happened that made you realize this was OCD, rather than something else?

_____

_____

_____

_____

ASSUMPTIONS AND BELIEFS

The assumptions and beliefs section of the formulation usually refers to some of the ideas we have about ourselves, other people and the world around us, as generated by our critical incident. When we go through any experience, we learn something about ourselves, those around us and the world we live in, and this is a common part of day-to-day living. However, when we experience our critical incident, we are likely to develop assumptions and beliefs that are directly related to the OCD. Assumptions tend to be what are known as 'if … then' statements e.g. 'If A happens then it means that B will happen'. By uncovering some of your own assumptions and beliefs, we are able to see what ideas you hold that may be maintaining your OCD, or keeping your OCD going.

Let's return to Adam's formulation to give you an example.

Case study: Adam

I developed a lot of assumptions when I moved to uni. My head was full of them. 'If I don't do the extra work then I'll fail', 'If I fail this assignment then uni will kick me out', 'If people know I am working extra hours then they will think I'm stupid'. I also have a lot of beliefs about other people. I think most people are cleverer than me. I think most people are naturally bright and achieve things easily. I think I make a lot of mistakes and that if I didn't check my work then people would think I was stupid. I think I am a bit stupid – I'm definitely not as clever as other people.

We can see from the above example that Adam has a lot of 'If … then …' statements in his formulation, as well as a lot of beliefs about how clever he is compared to other people. This lends a lot of insight into Adam's current OCD behaviour. If Adam genuinely believes that he is stupid and that others are much cleverer than he is, then this might explain his anxiety around making a mistake at work, and being judged by others. This in turn may explain his repeated checking of documents.

The rest of his formulation will show whether or not these ideas are correct.

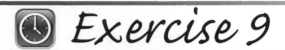

Exercise 9

For now, consider your own beliefs and assumptions. What beliefs do you hold about yourself, other people and the world you live in? What are your 'if ... then ...' statements? Take some time to consider these ideas and write your own response in the space below:

My beliefs about myself ...

_____

_____

_____

My beliefs about other people ...

_____

_____

_____

My beliefs about the world around me ...

_____

_____

_____

My assumptions/'if...then' statements ...

_____

_____

_____

INTRUSIVE THOUGHTS/IMAGES/URGES

In this part of the formulation, you consider how OCD is affecting you now. Specifically think about the 'obsessions', that is, the intrusive thoughts, urges and impulses you experience.

Let's return to Adam's formulation and see what he listed under his intrusions section:

'I'm stupid'

'I've done that wrong'

'What if I've made a mistake?'

'I'd better check it'

'If I don't check it then it will be the one time that it is wrong and then people will think I am incompetent'

'Check again. I haven't properly checked it. Repeated urges to check again and again … just in case'

Exercise 10

Consider the intrusive thoughts/images/urges you experience and describe them in the space below:

_____

_____

_____

_____

_____

_____

_____

➜ Creating a formulation

It is helpful to be able to map or draw out our formulation so that we can see how the different elements are linked.

Exercise 11

The diagram below is an example of what Adam's formulation looks like so far. Start to draw your own formulation out using the same headings – a blank formulation diagram has been included to help you.

Early experiences

(Making you vulnerable to OCD)
· Being told education is important
· Brother perceived as 'brighter'
· Can't tell anyone I'm struggling
· Secretive
· Negative family attitude
  towards laziness
· Long-term.

Critical incidents

(Starting this episode of OCD)
· Leaving home.

Activates.

Assumptions and beliefs

· If I don't do extra work then I'll fail
· If I fail then I'll be kicked out
· If people find out I'm working extra
  hours then they'll think I'm stupid.
· Other people are brighter than me.

Intrusive thoughts/images/urges/doubts.

· 'I'm stupid'   · 'What if I've made a mistake?'
· 'I've done that wrong'   · 'This will be the one time
· 'I'd better check it'   it's wrong.'
· Urge to check.

Early experiences

Critical incidents

Activates.

Assumptions and beliefs

Intrusive thoughts/images/urges/doubts.

Further copies of this Exercise can be found in the Appendix.

This part of our formulation so far can lead us to what therapists term the **vicious flower** formulation. The vicious flower refers to the actions that we think take us away and keep us safe from OCD but which actually draw us closer to OCD. There are several parts to consider that make up our vicious flower diagram and these are described below:

At the centre we have our misinterpretations of events, our appraisals and our beliefs about responsibility for events.

> *Misinterpretation of events, appraisal, responsibility.*

We then want to consider where our attention is in a situation. For example, in certain situations we may turn our attention inwards and be scanning our thoughts or our body looking for particular thoughts or physical symptoms. This is known as **attentional bias**.

While it may seem helpful initially, actually all it is doing is drawing attention to something that highlights our OCD thinking or beliefs rather than diminishes them. This means we are actually giving the OCD more attention and focus, by trying to distract from it.

Attentional bias

> *Misinterpretation of events, appraisal, responsibility.*

The next part to consider concerns any neutralizing actions. This may be mentally going over a sentence and replacing a thought or it may be reassurance-seeking, praying or completing a physical ritual such as checking, washing or counting.

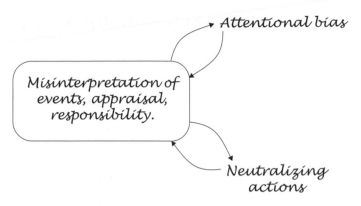

Emotional response is the next part of the vicious flower to consider. This refers to how you are feeling in the situation. While the typical response is anxiety, you may notice other related emotional responses such as feeling panicky, emotional, stressed, frustrated, angry or tearful.

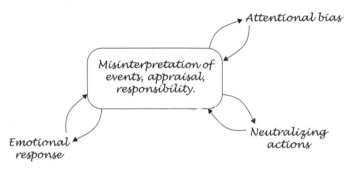

The final part is looking at your safety behaviours. These are things that you do that make you feel 'safe' from the OCD but that don't actually change or address anything about the OCD. A typical safety behaviour would be **avoidance**.

Avoidance means you prevent yourself being in, or thinking about, a certain situation. Often, people feel this is a good strategy as they can avoid the anxiety by avoiding the situation but this isn't curing the problem, and can make being in a particular situation that cannot be avoided feel very scary.

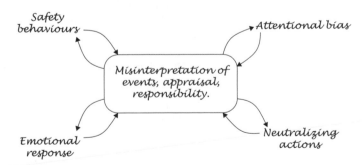

ADAM'S FORMULATION

Let's piece together all the elements for Adam's formulation

Looking at the diagram drawn out above using Adam's example, you can now see how the formulation fits together to paint a complete picture of the OCD. Now consider the blank diagram and complete your own formulation.

Early Experiences

(Making you vulnerable to OCD)
· *Being told education is important*
· *Brother perceived as 'brighter'*
· *Can't tell anyone I'm struggling*
· *Secretive*
· *Negative family attitude*
  towards laziness
· *Long-term.*

Critical Incident

(Starting this episode of OCD)
· *Leaving home.*

Activates.

Assumptions and beliefs

· *If I don't do extra work then I'll fail*
· *If I fail then I'll be kicked out*
· *If people find out I'm working extra*
  hours then they'll think I'm stupid.
· *Other people are brighter than me.*

Intrusive Thoughts/images/urges/doubts.

· *'I'm stupid'*
· *'I've done that wrong'*
· *'I'd better check it'*
· *Urge to check.*

· *'What if I've made a mistake?'*
· *'This will be the one time*
  it's wrong.'

Safety behaviours

· *Avoiding people @work*
· *Avoiding any increase in workload.*

Misinterpretation:
· *My work is full*
  of mistakes
· *I'm useless*
· *People will think*
  I'm stupid

Emotional response
· *Panic* · *Anxiety*
· *Fear*

Attentional bias

· *Looking for 'proof*
  of mistakes
· *'Scanning' work constantly*
· *Nervously watching for*
  others' reactions.

Neutralizing actions
· *Checking*
  documents
  at work

Early Experiences

Critical Incident

Activates.

Assumptions and beliefs

Intrusive thoughts, images, urges + doubts.

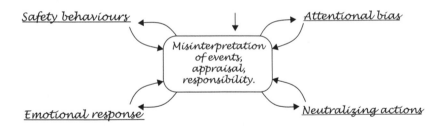

Safety behaviours

Attentional bias

Misinterpretation of events, appraisal, responsibility.

Emotional response

Neutralizing actions

By completing the above diagram you should now have a completed formulation and a good understanding of how and why your OCD developed, how it maintains itself and how it affects you today. Well done on completing your formulation – remember to keep this safe for regular review as you work your way through the book.

Key points to remember

▶ Formulation is a diagram that helps you to identify what led to your development of OCD.

▶ It is not a 'blame game'. Don't confuse recognizing what contributed to your OCD with blaming someone for you developing OCD.

▶ Your formulation is something that can be reviewed and updated throughout your therapy. It can also serve as a useful reference point to monitor progress.

▶ Sometimes it is helpful to write more than one formulation. Write out as many as you need to help you understand as many different aspects as you think will be helpful.

▶ If you think it will be helpful, speak to someone you trust who knows you well when writing your formulation as they will be able to help you write out your formulation, and make links between the past and the way things are now.

Where to next?

This chapter has shown you how to build the picture of your formulation. Through this process we have uncovered some of the thoughts and beliefs that underpin your OCD. The following chapter is designed to help you understand more about OCD thoughts (intrusions) and how to overcome them.

6

Understanding the nature of obsessions

About this chapter

▶ Previous chapters have helped you understand more about your OCD and how it developed. Now that you know what you are dealing with, this chapter is focusing on obsessions i.e. the intrusive thoughts/urges/images that you may experience.

▶ The chapter will talk you through the nature of obsessions and how an intrusive thought turns into OCD. You will also begin to examine your appraisal of your own obsessions. By gaining a clear understanding of your own obsessions we can then challenge and overcome them.

→ What is an obsession?

Typically the word 'obsession' refers to something that we are completely engaged with or can't stop thinking about in a positive way, such as 'I am completely obsessed with the new app on my phone!'. However, within the context of OCD, the word obsession refers to the intrusions we experience, which form part of having OCD.

Obsessions can take three forms:

INTRUSIVE THOUGHTS

These are words or questions that pop into our mind unbidden. For example, an intrusive thought may be 'are you sure that's right?' 'Did you just touch that?' 'That looks dirty', etc.

INTRUSIVE IMAGES

These are images or pictures that come into our mind out of the blue. For example, you may be talking to a colleague and suddenly have a picture of them naked pop into your mind, even though you are not attracted to them and the conversation is not related to that image in any way.

IMPULSES OR SUDDEN URGES

These impulses refer to when we suddenly feel an urge to do something but we're not sure why, and it's not something we particularly want to do. For example, we may be standing on a train platform and have an urge to push a child in front of a train, even though this isn't something we want to do, or would normally think about.

As you can see these obsessions all take different forms and it is common to experience all three types of obsessions with OCD.

The common factor with all these obsessions is that they are all intrusive. Intrusive means that they pop into our mind unbidden; we don't want to think about them. They are more often than not distressing in nature, either because we find the thought itself distressing, or because it evokes a great deal of anxiety within us which then consequently makes us distressed.

→ Common themes

As discussed earlier, OCD has a tendency to pick on something or someone that is important to you. This way you will pay attention to the intrusive thoughts and you will become a lot more anxious, which in turn, makes the OCD nice and strong.

So what exactly are we thinking about? There are several very common themes in OCD thinking, which people report having again and again. The most upsetting themes for people with OCD tend to be thoughts of a repugnant or 'disgusting' nature. These thoughts may include:

▶ Violent or harmful behaviour towards another person or child
  ▷ Thinking you have accidentally poisoned a family member
  ▷ Having an urge to drop a child or push someone over a balcony
  ▷ Doubting whether you hit someone or caused an accident when driving
▶ Sexual obsessions
  ▷ Intrusive thoughts about your sexuality/doubts about your sexual identity
  ▷ Images of committing a sexual act that goes against your character and/or beliefs e.g. sexual acts with children
  ▷ Urges to shout something sexually inappropriate at people/grope a stranger

- ▶ Religious obsessions
    - ▷ Urges to shout something blasphemous
    - ▷ Continual worries about good and evil and sinning
    - ▷ Doubts about honesty: 'was I absolutely truthful when I told a friend about my day? Did I leave out any details? Have I accidentally lied to them and been dishonest?'

The last obsession, concerning honesty, is often referred to as **scrupulosity**. This is a term that refers to extreme vigilance in keeping a very strict moral code. This is often out of sync with reality/what is reasonably expected by others. For example, does it really matter if you tell a friend that you turned left on to the road when actually it was right? Not especially (unless you are giving them directions!). However, for someone with scrupulosity, this would feel wilfully deceitful and dishonest and they may feel an urge to repeat the story from the start getting the details right, or neutralize their 'lying' in some way.

There are many other themes to obsessions, however the ones listed above are the most common. These are also, ironically, the types of thoughts that people think no one else has. People who come to see me for treatment often say 'What's wrong with me? Why am I thinking these thoughts when no one else is?'.

Actually, these obsessions are not only applicable to those with OCD. Research from the United States found that between 80–90 per cent of the people they asked, from various countries and backgrounds, including Britain, Canada and South Korea, have reported regular unwanted thoughts with these themes.

Remember with all this research, we can only report the people who were willing to admit to having these thoughts – my guess would be that actually 100 per cent of people have unwanted intrusive thoughts, around the topics and themes discussed above. However, those without OCD may not even notice such thoughts.

It is difficult to admit to these thoughts, and people do worry about the stigma that is attached to them, and how they will be perceived. This difficulty is often what prevents people from seeking help in the first place. After all, how do you walk into your GP and say 'I can't stop thinking about abusing my child?'. People are concerned about the reaction of others, and the possible consequences of admitting to a thought like this, and this prevents them from seeking help.

→ Everyone has these thoughts, even the horrid ones, so why doesn't everyone get OCD?

So, if everyone has these horrible, unwanted and intrusive thoughts, how come not everyone develops OCD? One of the principles of cognitive therapy, as outlined by Beck (1976), is that what happens to us doesn't actually matter, but the interpretation we give to what has happened does. Our interpretation can impact heavily on our mood and on our perception of events and how we feel about ourselves.

Example:

> Situation – about to leave the house when it starts to rain heavily
>
> Interpretation – 'oh great that's my day ruined. I'm the unluckiest person in the world'
>
> Mood – depressed and deflated, want to stay at home

Let's take the same situation again but this time give the situation a new interpretation

> Situation – about to leave the house when it starts to rain heavily
>
> Interpretation – 'Woohoo! Now I get to try out my gorgeous new umbrella!'
>
> Mood – happy and ready to get going

You can see in this example that the simple act of changing the interpretation and response to a situation had a big impact on mood and the outcome of the situation. Now exactly the same thing happens when we experience an intrusive thought. *It's not the thought itself that signifies OCD, but rather the meaning that we attach to it.*

Example: Susan is at the top of the stairs holding her 11-week-old baby. She suddenly experiences an intrusive image of opening her arms and watching her baby bounce down the stairs.

Appraisal 1: Susan dismisses this thought maybe thinking 'gosh that's an odd thought' but then carries on with her day.

Appraisal 2: 'Why would I think that?! I must be a horrible person. I'm dangerous. I shouldn't be holding my baby.'

As you can see, with the first appraisal Susan may recognize that thought but she quickly dismisses it and carries on. However, with the second appraisal, Susan interprets the thought/image as meaning something about her, e.g. 'I'm dangerous'. Susan also then thinks that she shouldn't be holding her baby. This is probably due to a feeling of 'just in case'.

A 'just in case' feeling is very common in OCD, and refers to how we may not believe we will do something but we prevent ourselves from being in that situation 'just in case' we do. For example, Susan may now feel trapped and overwhelmed and put her baby down/refuse to carry her near stairs/ask someone else to help her carry the baby. This would be a classic example of Susan interpreting her thoughts/images as meaning something about her.

This is the only difference between someone with OCD and someone without OCD experiencing the same thought. The person without OCD may not even register the thought, they will dismiss the thought easily, and they will not attribute a meaning to the thought. However, the person with OCD will interpret the thought as meaning something about them, and respond to that thought by changing their behaviour and experiencing high anxiety.

Exercise 13

Have a think about some of the thoughts that you notice in a typical day. Either go back to your formulation or monitor your thoughts over the next day or two, and write down the obsessions (thoughts/images/urges) that you experience and then write down your appraisal of them. A few examples have been given to help you below:

Intrusive thought/image/urge	Possible appraisal/Meaning given to that thought
Image of pushing someone in front of the train 'I might sexually abuse my child'	'I must be going mad. I shouldn't go on trains anymore.' 'I must be dangerous. I'm a bad person. I'm a terrible parent.'

Write your own obsessions here	Write your own appraisals here

→ What's the meaning behind the meaning?

Those with OCD not only spot a meaning behind their obsessional thought/image/urge as we've seen above, they also misinterpret a meaning behind the meaning. As we saw earlier with Susan's example, not only does she think the thought means something about her, she also thinks that something might happen and thus changes her behaviour accordingly.

Often these meanings behind the meanings fall into one of three categories:

1 'I'm mad' – there must be something wrong with me. I'm losing my mind. I must be crazy. It's not normal to think like this.

2 'I'm bad' – there must be something genuinely bad about my character. I'm evil. I'm a disgusting person. Good people don't have these thoughts and urges. I am a terrible person.

3 'I'm dangerous' – I can't be trusted. I might lose control and act on these obsessions. I need to stay away from people.

Sometimes we may feel that our obsessions fall into more than one of these categories. However, we can begin to see why thinking this about ourselves, and attaching this meaning to ourselves as well as the obsession, is so distressing and upsetting for those with OCD.

So as you can see it's the meaning or appraisal we give to an obsession that defines the OCD, not the obsession itself.

This idea is the underpinning of the CBT model of OCD as developed by Salkovskis (1996) and Rachman (1997). They propose that these misinterpretations of obsessions cause the development and maintenance of OCD to persist. See the diagram below:

🕐 *Exercise 14*

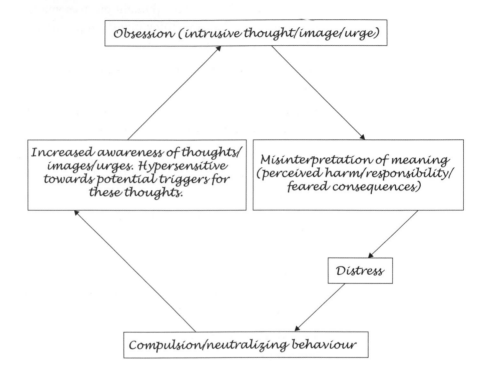

Looking at the model above, consider some of your own thoughts and behaviour and complete the CBT for OCD model for yourself. Work through the model using an example obsession that you struggle with and how this makes you feel.

Further copies of this Exercise can be found in the Appendix.

→ Getting to the root of the problem

Within OCD, we look at the beliefs and thoughts that may be underneath the obsessions we are having. We do this because in OCD often the obsessions are symptoms of an underlying fear or belief. If we can get to the underlying belief then we are able to challenge the cause of the OCD, rather than just treat the symptoms. To do this we continue to question the deeper meaning of our thoughts until we hit on the key thought/belief that we believe is maintaining our obsessions.

Below is an excerpt from a conversation I had with Simone regarding her obsessional fear of germs, which was leading to some extreme cleaning rituals. Read through the case study for an example of 'digging deeper' to get to the root of an obsession.

Case study: Simone

Me: Simone you have told me about some of the more extreme cleaning rituals you have been completing over the last few months, including the repeated cleaning and bleaching of your children's toys. When you are cleaning these toys, what's going through your mind?

Simone: Well say if I've unloaded the dishwasher and Jamie is behind me in the high chair and drops a toy and I pick it up I suddenly think 'what if there is dishwasher residue on my hands' and so I have to take the toy back off him and sterilize it. I often bleach the toy and then pour boiling water over it and then put it in the sterilizer. I had to get rid of the toys with batteries in because you can't put them in the sterilizer. He doesn't like it though because he'll be playing with a toy and I take it off him for a good ten minutes. By the time it's clean enough he'll be disinterested and not want it back.

Me: OK, so when you go through this cleaning process what's going through your mind?

Simone: If I don't do it then he'll eat some dishwasher residue.

Me: What's the worst thing about Jamie eating some dishwasher residue?

Simone: Well, he's only little and it might upset his tummy.

Me: What would the worst thing about upsetting his tummy be?

Simone: Well he might have ingested some chemicals and he might become really poorly.

Me: So when you say really poorly?

Simone: Well, you know, he might be sick, or get really sick, I might have to rush him to hospital?

Me: And what would be the worst thing about taking Jamie to hospital?

Simone: I guess there are two things really. Everyone would judge me and think I was a rubbish mum and the doctors might call social services and have him taken off me. The other thing is what if I didn't get there on time and he got really sick and died? That would be all my fault.

Me: So if we think about it, it sounds as though the fear isn't that you have to clean and bleach Jamie's toys because you think they are dirty. The deeper fear is that if you don't clean and sterilize his toys then you will be judged for being a bad mother and Jamie might die.

Simone: Yeah that's it. That's exactly it. I've never thought about it so directly before but you're right. Every time I hand him something at the back of my mind is the fear that I might kill him. Then I snatch it back and clean it.

Me: So would that make sense of why these obsessions are so troubling and why they won't go away? Because you are not experiencing the fear that the toy is dirty, you are actually experiencing the fear that your son may die.

Simone: Absolutely. My word – no wonder these thoughts are so scary! I seriously am thinking every time I do anything with him that I've somehow not done everything properly and that he's going to die.

So as you can see from the example above, when we keep questioning why something is bothering us, we are able to uncover the root of our belief and the deeper meaning of what we are thinking. This is helpful as we can uncover what we are actually anxious about and spot any thinking errors that we can then challenge.

⏱ *Exercise 15*

Use the space below to continue to dig deeper and try to get to the root of your OCD thinking. To help you, use the questions below as prompts and write down your answers to help you track your train of thought. Keep 'digging' until you feel you have hit on your core belief or worry that may be keeping your anxiety going.

What is the worst thing about that situation?

_____

_____

_____

_____

_____

What would other people's reactions be?

_____

_____

_____

_____

_____

What do you think might happen as a consequence?

_____

_____

_____

_____

_____

What is the worst thing about that?

_____

_____

_____

_____

_____

What is the ultimate fear in this situation?

_____

_____

_____

_____

_____

Use the space below to continue your thinking and digging. Once you have identified what you think of as your maintaining fears e.g. what is underlying the obsessions, draw a line under or highlight that thought/belief. We'll be coming back to it when we challenge our thinking later on.

_____

_____

_____

_____

_____

_____

_____

_____

Key points to remember

- ▶ Obsessions can take the form of intrusive thoughts, images and/or impulses.
- ▶ Everyone experiences intrusive thoughts, but not everyone develops OCD
- ▶ Those who develop OCD apply a meaning to the thought that is not accurate or true
- ▶ The interpretations tend to fall into one of three categories, which are 'mad', 'bad' or 'dangerous' or possibly all three
- ▶ We need to dig deeper to uncover the 'root' of our thinking and the beliefs that concern us.

Where to next?

This chapter has taught you more about your obsessions and helped you to uncover some of the deeper meanings behind your obsessions. The next chapter is going to focus on identifying and challenging thinking errors in OCD in order to start to overcome your obsessions. Get ready to start challenging your thinking!

7 Challenging your thinking

. . . .

About this chapter

▶ This chapter is going to talk you through thinking errors that are common in anxiety and specifically in OCD. You will then identify your own thinking errors and begin to challenge them. This chapter offers you specific ways of challenging your thinking and you will need time to complete the tasks, however they have been designed to fit into your everyday life.

. . . .

→ What are thinking errors?

Thinking errors are patterns of thinking that we can develop that skew the way we think about ourselves and the world around us. We are probably unaware of our thinking errors as they can become habitual, and we just start to think in a certain way, without realizing that we are doing so. However, identifying our thinking errors is important as there are certain ways of thinking that maintain our OCD and can make our OCD beliefs stronger. By being more aware we can change our thinking errors to develop a more 'typical' way of thinking, as opposed to an anxiety-driven approach.

The following sections talk you through anxiety and OCD-related thinking errors, and encourage you to identify and note down ones that you recognize. Keep a record of these as we will then move on to look at challenging them.

→ Common anxious-thinking errors
BLACK AND WHITE THINKING

This is also known as 'all or nothing' thinking, whereby people tend to think in extremes. For example, a situation can either be brilliant or awful, people can either be lovely or horrible, we can think of ourselves as perfect or the worst person ever. With black and white thinking there is no 'wriggle room' or grey area, instead we think in absolutes.

This also affects how we see situations and those around us. Black and white thinking within anxiety tends to be skewed towards the negative. This may mean that you have a lovely stay in a hotel all week, however on the very last day the receptionist is a bit off with you. When people ask you about the hotel afterwards you say 'well the hotel stay was really uncomfortable because the staff were very off and rude with us'. Our black and white thinking can become a blanket statement to cover our entire experience.

CATASTROPHIC THINKING

This is, as it sounds, thinking the worst or imagining a catastrophic outcome during seemingly everyday 'normal' experiences. This is particularly present within OCD – after all, OCD never tells you that everything is going to be fine now does it? Instead it is constantly encouraging catastrophic thinking meaning your thoughts and worries quickly escalate towards the worst case scenario.

MIND-READING

Mind-reading refers to thoughts where we predict others' responses or thoughts, for example, 'people will think I'm an idiot', 'people will look at me', 'people will know I'm nervous', 'that person doesn't like me and will think I'm weird'. When we mind-read we often think we know what other people's responses will be and find ourselves worrying or reacting to their predicted responses before an event takes place. For example, worrying that someone dislikes us because we think that they are thinking negatively about us.

DISQUALIFYING THE POSITIVE

This refers to the way we can dismiss or belittle positive achievements or experiences and not recognize our own role in these. For example, we may attribute success to luck rather than our own hard work, 'I was lucky to pass that exam'.

This kind of thinking usually only affects the positive events – we take the blame for the negative events in our lives but dismiss our role in and responsibility for the positive. So if something goes wrong then it's 'all our fault' but if something goes well then 'we were lucky'.

FILTERING

This is when we see the world through a negative or anxious filter, e.g. we are unable to see the positive or good things that happen around us – our minds start to focus only on the negative events or worries. For example, we may have given an outstanding presentation at work. While receiving congratulations and feedback a colleague says: 'That was brilliant! I thought you were going to mention XYZ project but I'm so glad you didn't because this was much better!'. Your inner-filter latches on to the idea that you didn't mention something that a colleague was expecting. You filter out the positive feedback and instead get caught up in what was 'missed'. This becomes the focus for you and you think negatively about the presentation and feel foolish and anxious, rather than remember the compliments and praise from others.

→ Thinking errors specific to OCD

The thinking errors discussed above refer to anxiety-provoking thinking errors that may affect us all. The thinking errors listed below are linked to intrusive thoughts. There are certain thinking errors that may make us more likely to carry out a compulsion. These thinking errors are beliefs that we hold about our thoughts that may make it more compelling to neutralize the obsessions, or try to counteract it in some way.

Exercise 16

Have a look at the thinking errors explained below. In the space beneath each explanation, consider if you hold this thinking error. If so, use the space to identify and write in your own experience of this thinking error, how it makes you feel, and what you do as a result of it. Continue to do this throughout all the explanations given below:

Now I've thought about it it's more likely to happen ... This idea is termed **thought-action fusion** (Rachman and Shafran, 1999) and refers to the idea that by thinking about something happening we are more likely to make it happen. This idea also refers to a belief that thinking about doing something is as 'bad' as actually doing it.

For example, thinking about stealing some chocolate from the shop is equivalent to actually stealing it (Rachman and Shafran, 1999). Thinking this way may cause us a lot of distress and guilt, and may lead us to carry out some neutralizing compulsion to try to wipe out or undo the thought or image.

Yes this happens to me/No this doesn't sound like me (delete as applicable)

If 'yes', then write your experience of this here:

_____

_____

_____

_____

_____

_____

_____

_____

_____

Now I have thought about it, it is my responsibility ... This idea is also known as **inflated responsibility**, a concept introduced by Salkovskis (1996) and is one of the most common ideas underpinning OCD.

Inflated responsibility is a belief that if you have thought of something and can perceive negative consequences happening, then you are responsible for preventing that happening, even if it doesn't directly relate to you.

For example, you are walking along the pavement to collect your children from school and you notice some glass in the road. You may have the intrusive image of a car going over the glass, bursting a tyre and losing control, possibly driving into the school and hurting children in the process. Now that you have had this thought, if you had inflated responsibility you may feel that you now have to do something to prevent that happening e.g. you feel responsible for the outcome of that glass, and will try to move the glass. This is despite the fact that you did not smash the glass or leave it in the road in the first place. By thinking about it, and 'realizing' the potential negative consequence, you now feel responsible for doing something about it. By not clearing the glass you may feel accountable and perhaps even liable for any negative consequences that occur as a result. This may lead to acute distress and a compulsion to do something about it.

Yes this happens to me/No this doesn't sound like me (delete as applicable)

If 'yes', then write your experience of this here:

_____

_____

_____

_____

_____

_____

_____

_____

_____

_____

There is a right way to do things and I should try to do it that way ... this belief is commonly referred to as **perfectionism** and refers to a belief that there is a correct way of behaving/doing/thinking and that one should try to only do things in that correct way. It can be quite common with perfectionism for people to feel they must try to do things 'perfectly' and that if they don't there will be negative consequences as a result. While there is nothing wrong with striving for excellence, perfection is unrealistic and unattainable. This is because your OCD will always find something that you could have done better or 'more perfectly'.

This is why those with perfectionism are rarely satisfied and almost never feel as though they have achieved what they wanted to. Sometimes perfectionists cannot prioritize their tasks as they think everything should be done perfectly. This can cause a great deal of delay and disruption to their day as rather than quickly replying to an email, they may have to review it over and over and over again, checking that it is perfect.

Those with perfectionism often take much longer over seemingly simple tasks, and struggle to do things any other way. Those with perfectionism would rather not do things at all if they cannot do them perfectly. Those with perfectionism tend to do things out of fear of failing to meet these standards rather than for the satisfaction they gain from doing things a certain way.

Yes this happens to me/No this doesn't sound like me (delete as applicable)

If 'yes', then write your experience of this here:

_____

_____

_____

_____

_____

_____

_____

_____

I need to KNOW that this is ok now … This idea refers to an intolerance of uncertainty. **Intolerance of uncertainty** is one of the most common issues that I see in those with OCD. As the name suggests, intolerance of uncertainty refers to a belief that you need absolute certainty about a situation before you can move on with your day or complete what you are doing.

Case study: Sinead

Sinead is in a meeting and is watching a presentation that her boss is giving. At the end of the presentation she asks a question about one of the points made. Her boss answers the question and then the meeting carries on. Sinead suddenly gets an intrusive thought 'does my boss think I was criticizing her presentation?'. Sinead begins to worry that her boss is thinking that maybe Sinead was implying that her presentation was unclear and that she was trying to make a fool of her in front of the team (NB: notice the mind-reading). Sinead becomes uncomfortable and distressed and spends the rest of the meeting trying to read her boss's expression to see if she looks cross or upset with her.

Sinead cannot tolerate not knowing whether or not her boss is angry with her and so approaches her after the meeting and asks her if she is angry with her (reassurance seeking). Sinead is now so uncomfortable that actually she almost doesn't care if her boss is angry with her, she just needs to know. She cannot tolerate the uncertainty.

Yes this happens to me/No this doesn't sound like me (delete as applicable)

If 'yes', then write your experience of this here:

_____

_____

_____

_____

_____

_____

_____

_____

_____

_____

I think something terrible will happen now … This idea refers to the overestimation of threat in OCD. Often, people believe that something catastrophic will happen (after all, OCD rarely tells you that everything will be just fine!). This means that imagined consequences are often a lot more serious or severe than they are actually likely to be.

Case study: Judy

Judy gets into her car to go to work and her car doesn't start the first time. Judy immediately thinks 'oh my word I'll be late. I'll get told off, I might even get sacked, and then I won't be able to pay my mortgage. I'm going to be homeless'.

You can see here how Judy's OCD overestimated the consequence of her car not starting and immediately gave her a catastrophic outcome. It is very common for those with OCD to imagine the worst-case scenario and very quickly. For example, Judy's car may actually start the second time she tries it, but before that she has already imagined, and become distressed by, the worst-case scenario.

It is very common for those with OCD to overestimate the threat in a possible outcome, and to become distressed by this, despite the fact it may be unrealistic and may never happen.

Yes this happens to me/No this doesn't sound like me (delete as applicable)

If 'yes', then write your experience of this here:

_____

_____

_____

_____

_____

_____

_____

_____

_____

I must control my thoughts ... This idea refers **mental control**, which is a belief that we must control what we think and avoid thinking about certain things. This is particularly relevant to those with **thought-action fusion**, who believe that thinking something makes it more likely to happen. However, those who try to exert mental control over their thoughts may also feel as though controlling their thoughts makes them less likely to do something.

For example, if you have a thought that you might run someone over, you may hold a belief that you need to control these thoughts. By controlling them you may feel less likely to act on them. This is often true for those with OCD, who fear they may suddenly 'crack' or lose control and act on these thoughts even though they don't want to. As well as mental control, people may try to remove external stimuli that may prompt these thoughts. For example, if you hold a fear of stabbing someone, then you may remove all knives in an attempt to stop you thinking about it, and thus making you more likely to have and act on these thoughts.

Yes this happens to me/No this doesn't sound like me (delete as applicable)

If 'yes', then write your experience of this here:

_____

_____

_____

_____

_____

_____

_____

_____

_____

_____

➜ Need a clear picture of what we are dealing with

As you can see, thinking errors can be incredibly anxiety-provoking. The way that we think can affect our responses and how we deal with situations. In therapy, we need to get a really clear picture of the types of thoughts you are experiencing with your OCD. We do this using a **thought record**, which is a way of monitoring our thinking.

➜ But I think all the time!

The thought of monitoring your thinking may feel totally overwhelming, particularly as when we feel anxious, we can feel as though our mind 'races' and the idea of trying to record all those racing thoughts may feel impossible. However, in this task you are not having to write down every single thought that enters your head. Instead, we are looking at the thoughts that you have in different situations. Where you felt the OCD was present, or where you felt very anxious. In therapy we use a thought record, which has been drawn out for you below. Blank copies are also available in the Appendix.

However, for those on the go, who may not feel as though they want to carry around this workbook, I would suggest photocopying or drawing out the thought record to make it more portable. Individuals I work with often now enter the headings into their smartphones or laptops/tablets so that they can appear to be doing something else when completing their therapy homework. It doesn't really matter how you record your thoughts, the important aspect is that you are keeping a thought record, which can then be reviewed later on.

➜ Getting started

Exercise 17

Start your thought record by entering information under each of the columns. It is best to complete a column during or as soon after an event as you can, as this way the thoughts are easier to remember and we are able to record our thoughts more accurately.

Situation (where I was and what I was doing)	Thoughts I had in this situation	How I felt/what I did
e.g. At work at my desk, about to send an email	'I can't send this' 'It's full of mistakes' 'Everyone will think I'm incompetent and I'll lose my job'	Sent the email much later after I had checked it several times. In total I checked the email about 9-10 times. I briefly felt better that I'd checked it but very anxious that it was so late.

How long do I monitor my thoughts for?

We would usually recommend monitoring your thoughts for a week. When monitoring our thoughts, we want to monitor them for long enough to get a clear picture of what our OCD looks like. Imagine if you had to give someone this as an example of what it was like to have OCD, and to show them the sorts of thoughts and feelings you were experiencing. I talk to those I work with about 'giving me a slice of your OCD' so that it gives me some idea of what life is like for them day to day.

Draw out the columns in your therapy notebook and complete the diary for at least a week, or until you feel you have a good representation of your OCD thoughts and related feelings/behaviours.

Let's spot the errors!

OK, so as mentioned above, those with OCD have a tendency towards anxiety-provoking thinking errors. This means when we look carefully at our thoughts we can begin to spot some of these thinking errors and see them for what they are.

Look back over your thought record now and see if you can spot any thinking errors. An example of this reviewing process has been given below.

Situation (where I was and what I was doing)	Thoughts I had in this situation	How I felt/what I did	Thinking error?
e.g. At work at my desk, about to send an email	'I can't send this' 'It's full of mistakes' 'Everyone will think I'm incompetent and I'll lose my job'	Sent the email much later after I had checked it several times. In total I checked the email about 9-10 times. I briefly felt better that I'd checked it but very anxious that it was so late.	Mind reading – e.g. everyone will think I'm incompetent. Catastrophic thinking – e.g. I'll lose my job

→ Looking for evidence

Evidence is the biggest and most powerful weapon we have against OCD. OCD presents information to us as though it were fact. For example, OCD will not offer you a balanced view of something, instead it will just present something to you as a fait accompli. Therefore, when we are looking to overcome OCD, we need to stop trusting what OCD tells us – after all, we know that OCD is a bully and a liar. Instead we need to focus on gathering some evidence, before we decide what to do next.

If we consider the example from the thought record above, OCD is telling this person that their work is full of mistakes and that they need to repeatedly check it. However, OCD is presenting both these elements as fact. So what we would want to do instead of checking (which is, after all, just an OCD maintaining behaviour) is to seek evidence for and against the OCD ideas and then decide what we want to do.

When we talk about looking for evidence in therapy it is as though we are taking our thoughts to court. This means that we need concrete, factual, hard evidence. Thinking errors such as mind-reading, guessing, biases, stereotypes, etc. do not count. You need strong evidence for and against something, the kind of evidence that would stand up in a court of law.

Let's talk through an example of this to give you an idea, before you start evidence-seeking the ideas of your own:

OCD 'fact': 'This email is full of mistakes and I can't send it. Everyone will think I'm incompetent and I'll lose my job.'

Evidence for this:

I don't have any evidence for this other than the thought and anxiety itself, which is not fact, simply OCD.

Evidence against this:

▶ The wriggly red line that indicates spelling mistakes did not appear so the computer hasn't spotted any mistakes.

▶ I don't know what other people will think – I'm not a mind reader.

▶ I'm not incompetent. I am good at my job, as evidenced by my last work-performance appraisal.

▶ The email isn't even that important – no-one is probably going to read it that closely anyway. Even if I have made a mistake no one else would even notice.

▶ Other people make mistakes all the time and nothing bad happens to them.

▶ I can't be sacked for making a single mistake on an email anyway – that would be ridiculous!

Ok, so now we have noticed the thought and reviewed the evidence for it, we then make a decision about whether or not to act on the thought. Based on the evidence above, it is clear that the email doesn't need to be checked and so it can be sent without any further checking being carried out.

If we think back to our formulation at the beginning and the CBT model of how our thoughts, feelings, behaviours and physical symptoms all interact, then we can see how this analysis of the thought changes things. *Rather than just believing the thought and acting accordingly we stop and look for the evidence. Once we have gathered the evidence for and against the thought we can then behave in line with the evidence rather than other thoughts.*

Exercise 18

Do this yourself.

Look over your thought record and start to look for the evidence for and the evidence against your thoughts. Then ask yourself if you would change your behaviour/still act in the same way accordingly. Notice how looking for actual evidence changes the thought entirely, and notice how often OCD lies to us and makes us anxious over things that simply aren't true. Yet more proof of what a horrible lying bully OCD is! Keep a record of all your new information, thoughts and behaviours as a consequence of the new evidence-gathering. We'll continue to look at this in the next chapter.

Where to next?

This chapter has talked you through what thinking errors are and how to identify your own errors and OCD thinking. We have also looked at thought records and examining evidence for and against our thoughts in order to change our response to OCD. The next chapter continues to look at ways of challenging OCD thinking and deeper-held beliefs that may be maintaining your OCD.

8 Challenging OCD beliefs

About this chapter

▶ This chapter is going to talk you through ways of challenging your OCD thinking and the beliefs that underlie this thinking. By learning how to challenge the OCD beliefs you are starting to gain a more realistic perspective of yourself and the world around you, as opposed to the blinkered focus that OCD has given you. This chapter focuses on very practical techniques and gives examples in order to help you challenge your OCD beliefs.

→ ## Theory A versus Theory B

As previously described, OCD presents thoughts and ideas to us as facts. We know enough about OCD now to know that these 'facts' are just anxious thoughts that OCD convinces us are real so that we act on them and maintain the OCD. By accepting these 'facts' from OCD we won't ever question or challenge them, meaning we are constantly living in a state of anxiety. Therefore it is important to be able to question the ideas that OCD gives us and consider an alternative viewpoint, before we act on the thoughts.

Let's look at an example of this below:

Imagine you are walking down your road and you see your colleague Claire on the other side. You like Claire and so call after her 'Claire!' and smile and wave. Claire turns around, looks in your direction but does not smile or wave back. Instead she turns back and continues walking, leaving you standing there.

Let's take a moment to think about some of the interpretations we could put on this situation.

1 'Claire doesn't like me after all. I must have offended or upset her in some way and now she is ignoring me.'

2 'Claire was trying to embarrass me. She deliberately ignored me so I stood there looking foolish.'

3 'Claire is not my friend after all and doesn't want anything to do with me.'

These negative interpretations are the types of interpretation that OCD can give us in a specific situation. However, let's fast forward to the next day in the office. You bump into Claire and you decide to ask her if everything is alright as you are anxious that you might have upset or offended her. Claire looks surprised and says 'Why would I be upset? I did hear someone call my name but I didn't have my glasses on, and so when I turned around I couldn't see who it was and had to keep walking. I hope I didn't upset you'.

So not only was OCD wrong about you upsetting Claire, now Claire is worried she has upset you!

It is easy to see that in this situation it was not that Claire was ignoring you that was the problem, but rather the worry that she might be. *It was the anxiety provoked by the idea that she was ignoring you that caused the problem and anxiety, as opposed to the situation itself.*

Think back to the beginning of this workbook when we examined the theory behind OCD, and how it is our misinterpretation of events that leads to the development of OCD and anxiety, as opposed to the event itself. This is another example of how OCD thinking leads us to misinterpret situations and causes anxiety and worry. So we need to think of a logical way to challenge this OCD thinking and be able to interpret the situation more accurately, without OCD getting in the way.

This is the main thinking behind 'Theory A versus Theory B' (Salkovskis, 1999). This technique is commonly used in therapy to help people distinguish between what OCD is telling them and what is actually happening in a situation. By using Theory A versus Theory B we are able to challenge the thoughts that are maintaining our OCD. When we are in a situation we can have two theories:

Theory A – what OCD tells you is wrong about a situation

and

Theory B – what is actually wrong in a situation

Take a moment to distinguish between the two as it is important to understand the difference.

Let's look at the example below to help:

Situation: Unloading dishwasher

Theory A: (what OCD tells you): My problem is that there may be dishwasher tablet residue left on the dishes and I may poison my family.

Theory B: My problem is that I have OCD so even though I am a very careful person I am terrified about harming my family, and this causes me to worry about the dishwasher. The problem is not that the dishwasher is dangerous, the problem is that OCD tells me that it is and causes me anxiety.

Can you spot the distinction? It is not the dishwasher itself that causes any kind of problem, rather it is the worry that you have because you do not wish to harm your family. By recognizing the difference between the two theories, you will be able to challenge the ideas that are underlying some of your biggest OCD beliefs, and as such reduce your anxiety.

HOW DO I CHALLENGE THEORY A?

The most important step in challenging Theory A is to accept that your OCD might be wrong. As OCD presents ideas to us as absolute facts and we immediately react with anxiety, we never stop to think or challenge the OCD. So therefore the first step is to notice when OCD is giving you an interpretation of the situation and stop to think.

Exercise 19

Think of the last time you felt anxious because of OCD. What was OCD telling you? What interpretation did OCD give you about that situation? Take some time to consider this and write it in the space below. (It may be helpful to use your thought records from the previous chapter to act as a prompt.):

Situation	What OCD told me about the situation e.g. Theory A	How I felt in that situation	How I responded in that situation

Now reconsider the situation. Think about what it was that you were actually worried about. Was it the situation itself that was the problem or was it the worry that the situation caused that became the problem?

Pitfall! Sometimes people say to me that it is the situation that is the problem as without the situation they wouldn't worry – but it is important not to get too caught up in this idea. Remember we can get caught up in worries about situations that are everyday and innocuous. We cannot avoid all situations in case they cause us anxiety. In this sense it is not the situation that is the problem but rather it is the OCD.

 *Exercise 20*

Reconsider the situation now and complete the table below. What might be an alternative (Theory B) thought about the situation? (An example has been given as a prompt.)

Situation	Theory A (what OCD told me was the problem)	Theory B (what actually was the problem)
e.g. Emptying dishwasher	There may be dishwasher tablet residue left on the dishes and I may poison my family	I have OCD, and this is telling me that there is a problem with the dishwasher. I am a very careful person who is terrified of harming my family, and this makes me listen to the worry about the dishwasher.

Consider how you recorded reacting to Theory A. Now consider that if Theory B were true, and you were able to see that this was OCD playing a horrible trick on you, how this would change your own reaction and what you might do in that situation. We know that our thoughts, feelings, behaviours and physical symptoms all interact and so by changing how we are thinking about a situation, this will affect our level of anxiety and what we feel we 'have' to do.

 Exercise 21

Let's start using the strategies we have learned so far to challenge the OCD thinking and complete the Theory A versus Theory B table below. The earlier example has been continued to help you. Once you have read through the example, then complete the table working through some of your own OCD thoughts.

Theory A	Theory B
There may be dishwasher tablet residue left on the dishes and I may poison my family.	*I have OCD, and this is telling me that there is a problem with the dishwasher. I am a very careful person who is terrified of harming my family, and this makes me listen to the worry about the dishwasher.*
Evidence	**Evidence**
I once noticed that the dishwasher tablet hadn't completely dissolved in a friend's dishwasher.	*I use my dishwasher every day and have never noticed a problem.* *They wouldn't be allowed to sell dishwasher tablets if they were really dangerous/so hazardous to human health when used properly.* *I have worried about similar anxieties before and they turned out to be false.*

If this is true what do I need to do?	If this is true what do I need to do?
Check the dishwasher tablet has dissolved every time. Rinse every object out of the dishwasher. Stop using the dishwasher. Throw out the appliance. Stop eating out at restaurants where they use dishwashers. Stay in and never leave the house.	Recognize that this is OCD and not respond to the thoughts. Challenge the thought. Tolerate the anxiety and deliberately challenge the OCD.
What does this say about the future?	What does this say about the future?
My OCD will continue to rule my life. I will feel so anxious I won't be able to do anything that I want to do. I will have to continue to check everything in case it's dangerous.	Anxiety will reduce. I can stop worrying about this. Other worries will be less scary as I will recognize them as just being OCD and not a real threat.
What does this say about me as a person?	What does this say about me as a person?
I'm careless and irresponsible if I ignore this danger.	I care about my family a great deal and know I need to beat this for all of us to be happier.

Now that you have read through the example, complete the table below.

Tip: You may want to complete this several times in order to tackle different types of OCD worries. Also, if you struggle to complete this, maybe ask a trusted friend or colleague to help you gain an objective viewpoint.

Theory A	Theory B
Evidence	**Evidence**
If this is true what do I need to do?	**If this is true what do I need to do?**
What does this say about the future?	**What does this say about the future?**
What does this say about me as a person?	**What does this say about me as a person?**

USING BEHAVIOURAL EXPERIMENTS TO GAIN EVIDENCE FOR THEORY A VERSUS THEORY B

Behavioural experiments are a way for us to gain evidence that we can use to challenge our OCD thinking and behaviours.

Step 1 – identifying the 'key' cognition or belief to be tested.

The first step in setting up a behavioural experiment is to identify the specific thought or belief that you are going to test. You could use previous thought records to help you. Identify a key thought or belief that you feel is problematic, and use this as the basis of your behavioural experiment.

Step 2 – rate the belief (0–100%)

Once you have identified the thought that you need to test out then you need to rate how strongly you believe that thought out of 100%.

Step 3 – plan the experiment

Now that you have identified the exact thought or belief to be tested, and you have rated that thought, you need to plan a way of testing this out.

Key points to remember when planning:

▶ The experiment needs to be long enough to provide a fair test. Your experiment needs to have a realistic timeframe to provide an accurate test of the thought (e.g. not checking for 1 second is not a real test of whether or not you are safe to stop checking).

▶ The experiment needs to be do able and realistic. There is no point setting yourself a behavioural experiment so challenging that you are unable to complete it. A quick way to test this is to ask yourself how likely on a scale of 1–10 are you to complete this? If the answer is anything less than 7 then it is unlikely that you will go ahead. Adjust the timing or the situation enough to make it more comfortable. BUT …

▶ … don't make it too easy. If you are testing something out and it doesn't feel challenging or difficult in any way then it is unlikely that you are testing something significant or 'key' to your OCD.

USING A BEHAVIOURAL EXPERIMENT WORKSHEET

Whenever we complete a behavioural experiment we are mainly interested in three things.

1 What do you think will happen?

2 What did happen?

3 How did you feel afterwards?

 *Exercise 22*

If you are unable to complete a full behavioural experiment worksheet in a situation then ask yourself those three questions in any situation where you try to challenge a thought or belief.

The behavioural experiment worksheet below is a more comprehensive way of completing and evaluating behavioural experiments.

Date and situation	*Write down in detail here when and where you were, who you were with etc.*	
Key thought being tested/What do you think will happen?	*Write down your key cognition/belief that is going to be tested here. Rate how strongly you believe this thought/belief at the time. (%)*	

What did happen?	Write down here what happened during the experiment.	
How do you feel now?	Write here how you feel now and anything that you weren't expecting or that surprised you.	
Re-rated key thought	Re-evaluate that initial key thought/belief and re-rate how strongly you believe that thought/belief now (%).	

→ Further strategies for challenging OCD

Challenging the belief: 'I'm an XYZ type of person.'

Case study: Monica

When Monica became pregnant with her first child she was overjoyed as she had wanted to have a child for a long time. As time went on, Monica found it hard to come to terms with the changes in her body and she felt exhausted and run down throughout her pregnancy. When her baby, Christine, was born, Monica found that she was difficult to soothe and would often be awake all through the night. Monica became more and more exhausted and one day leaning over the cot she had the thought: 'I wish I'd never had my baby.' Monica was horrified by this thought and immediately worried that if she thought that then her baby might die and so whenever she had that thought she would say out loud: 'I love my baby very much I don't want her to die.'

Monica started to distract herself and would tell everyone around her how much she loved being a mother and how much she loved her baby. Monica began to worry about her thoughts and felt she was a bad mother. Monica developed a series of rituals in her head which she went through to neutralize the thoughts, including praying her baby would live, trying to replace all negative thoughts with positive thoughts and repeatedly saying phrases over and over in her mind when with her baby. Monica did not share her thoughts with anyone as she believed she was a bad mother and that Christine would be taken away from her.

→ Challenging the beliefs: let's put it on a scale

If you are struggling with the idea of being a bad person then create a scale. Think of two people, one whom you would consider a bad person and one whom you would consider a good person. These could either be people you know or celebrities/famous people.

Then mark on the scale where you think you are. Then consider all the evidence (remember actual evidence that would stand up in court – thoughts don't count!) and re-evaluate your beliefs about yourself as a person. Do you really belong where you have put yourself? Most of us won't belong at one extreme or the other – we sit somewhere in between. Use other people you know as a point of reference.

NB: It is very important when making our mark on the scale that we remember contexts. For example, if we had a scale of calm—angry, then we may feel that we are relatively calm and therefore be marked quite low on the scale. However, if someone cuts us up in traffic and nearly hits our car, we might feel very angry towards the other driver and in that situation we may shoot up the scale to the very extreme of anger.

Being made angry by a reckless driver does not mean that we are a mad, bad or dangerous person. Sometimes OCD can make us believe that we need to maintain a constantly neutral state but as we do not live in a world that is constant this just isn't possible, or necessary.

Therefore don't be afraid of feeling negative emotion. You are allowed to feel angry, upset, furious, annoyed and emotional in different contexts. If we react to a situation and feel a certain way in one context, it does not follow that that is who we are in every situation.

🕐 Exercise 23

Think of different scenarios and different contexts and rate yourself on different scales across these. Begin to notice how you are different in different contexts. Use this to challenge the idea that you are a 'mad, bad or dangerous' person. It is quite possible to feel strong emotion in one context but not in another and this doesn't make you a bad person.

_____

_____

_____

_____

_____

_____

→ Our survey says...

Using a survey is an incredibly effective way to challenge an OCD belief, particularly if we hold a belief that our thinking isn't 'normal' or that we are the only ones who think this way.

Often, people will say to me that they do not know whether something is a justifiable worry or whether it is OCD. This often becomes even harder with OCD as it can affect our confidence in our own decision-making, and so we begin to doubt our ability to judge a situation accurately. This is where seeking the opinion of others can be so helpful.

There are a few simple rules to remember when conducting a survey:

1   Ask people whose opinion you care about. There is no point conducting a survey of people if you don't value their opinions. OCD will quickly find a way to disqualify their answers if they are not meaningful to you, so make sure that you ask significant people.

2   Don't be coy. If you want a straightforward answer then ask a straightforward question. Remember there is no place for mind-reading or second-guessing, so make sure you ask the question you want the answer to.

3   Ask for help if it's too much. If you feel too shy to conduct the survey yourself, or you are not too sure who to ask, then enlist the help of a partner, friend or colleague. Surveys can be given out and completed anonymously, and often this encourages people to participate honestly.

4 Get as many results as you need. If you feel that a handful of friends answering your survey isn't enough then take advantage of social media. Many survey sites are available online where you can set up a simple online survey for free, and often they will even analyse the results for you e.g. X% of people agree with this statement, etc. This can be really helpful so take advantage of today's social media and post your survey wherever you feel you will get the most responses.

Be aware of the survey screening bias. Review the results accurately and not through an OCD filter. For example, if 99 per cent of responses agree with you and 1 per cent agrees with your OCD then it is important to recognize that it is you who is correct and not your OCD.

Also, let's not forget that you are not alone with OCD and so that 1 per cent may in fact be someone else's OCD which is agreeing with your OCD!

→ I will go mad and lose control

Often, underneath an anxiety about a situation is a fear that we will somehow lose control of ourselves and 'go mad'. This can be frightening on many levels.

▶ First, we may stop trusting ourselves.

▶ Second, we may feel that the more we think about something then the more likely we are to make it happen (see the chapter on thought-action fusion).

▶ Third, we may feel that we are actually losing control of our own minds and bodies. This may then make it feel more likely that we will somehow 'go mad' and cause a big scene or do something 'terrible' in public/in a specific situation. We can then start to worry about the consequences of such a situation and become so anxious that we cannot entertain the thoughts, let alone face the situation itself.

All of these feelings can be intensely frightening and extremely debilitating as they may stop us doing and achieving what we want to do. They may also affect our ability to try something new or take on a new challenge, and we may retreat further into ourselves for fear of being seen as 'mad'.

WHAT DO YOU MEAN BY 'MAD'?

Often when I talk to people about what they fear might happen in a certain situation they say to me something like 'I'll be in the middle of the situation and I'll be really anxious and I won't be able to escape and I'll just lose the plot/go mad/lose control'. However, when we pick this apart it becomes clear that although people think they will 'go mad' in a situation they don't actually have a clear picture of what that looks like. It's as though OCD plays a DVD in our minds of us in a situation but then when it gets to the bit where we lose control, or 'go mad', the DVD stops and the screen loses focus.

PLAY THE DVD ON ...

Using this analogy, try to encourage the DVD to continue playing. Ask yourself:

▶ What would actually happen if I 'went mad'?

▶ What do I think I would be doing?

▶ What would I look like?

▶ What would other people around me be doing?

▶ How would they be reacting?

Consider the situation realistically. If someone was behaving like that in front of you, how would you respond to them?

 *Exercise 24*

Think of the scenario that you picture when you think of losing control. Keep 'digging' in this scenario until you uncover what your biggest fear is. Then challenge it. Ask yourself:

How likely is this to happen?

_____

_____

_____

_____

Is my worst case scenario actually probable?

_____

_____

_____

_____

Would I react like that if someone were acting this way in front of me?

_____

_____

_____

_____

If the worst did happen, then could I recover from it?

_____

_____

_____

_____

What evidence do I have that this is ever likely to happen to me?

_____

_____

_____

_____

Keep a record of your responses and check them for OCD thinking errors. Are you guessing at the outcome? Could you break this down into smaller behavioural experiments to gain some evidence? By thinking about this logically we can eliminate the idea of 'going mad' and can build our confidence that we won't lose control in different situations.

 *Exercise 25*

A quick behavioural experiment to try is to get someone you know (and trust!) to sit on a chair and hold a glass of water over their head. Then think over and over and over again about tipping the glass of water over them but don't do it. Even though you think about it continually there will be something that inhibits you and you won't tip the water over them. Use this as evidence that you can act independently of your thoughts.

How avoidance is strengthening your OCD

Avoidance can feel as though it is preventing you from becoming anxious, and so can feel positive. However, avoidance actually *maintains* OCD. This is because by avoiding certain situations, we never get an opportunity to disconfirm the beliefs we hold about that situation. Continually avoiding means that we never gather any evidence for or against that belief and so we continue to hold on to an unhelpful OCD belief.

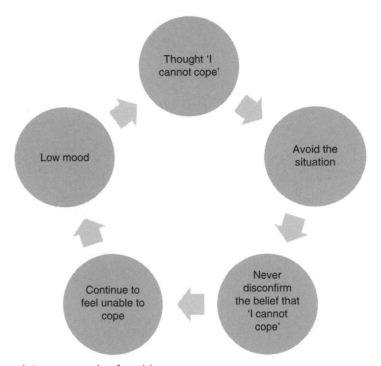

The maintenance cycle of avoidance

Every time you avoid something you are adding a little bit of strength to the idea that your OCD thinking is correct. Because of this, the longer you avoid, the harder it can feel to face the situation, as the OCD will have been strengthened.

Understanding the peaks of anxiety

If you feel anxious, it is a common experience to feel as though your anxiety is going up and up and may never stop, and so we picture our anxiety continuing forever, as shown below:

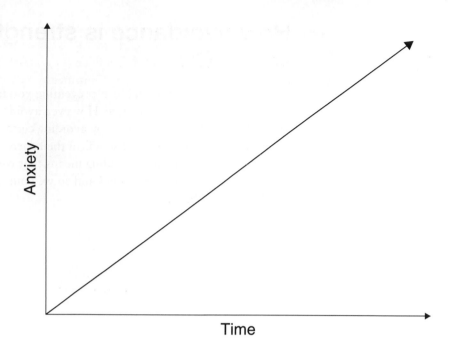

When we avoid a situation we cut that anxiety short as we escape the situation that is making us anxious and so our anxiety is immediately reduced:

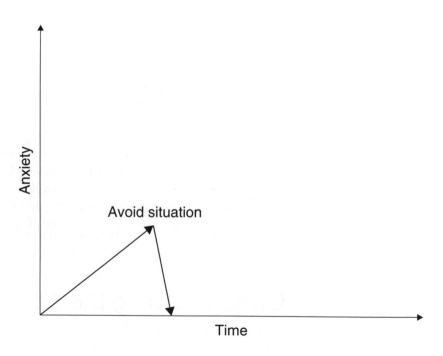

However, this anxiety is only temporarily reduced, and avoiding the situation makes it that much harder to go back into at another time since avoiding makes us lose confidence in ourselves and so the anxiety comes back stronger every time. This means we can experience anxiety in ever-increasing peaks and avoidance may not be as effective at reducing our anxiety:

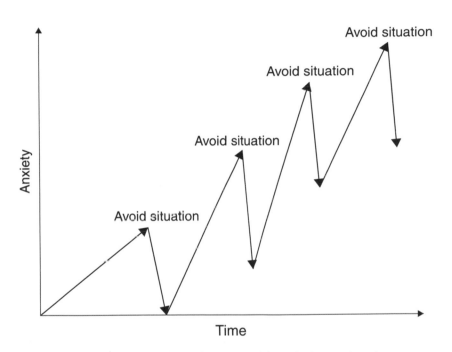

As you can see from the above diagram, although the anxiety is reduced, this reduction is temporary and the initial anxiety levels are much higher to begin with. We tend to avoid and escape situations as soon as we feel anxious.

The same can be said for checking. If we feel the anxiety rise we go back to check a situation or gather reassurance, meaning we are 'avoiding' challenging the OCD.

However, anxiety does not continue increasing forever and ever. Our bodies are designed to limit and reduce anxiety naturally over a period of about 20–25 minutes. This means that if we stay in the situation rather than immediately escape to check or avoid, our anxiety would naturally reduce and we would feel less anxious:

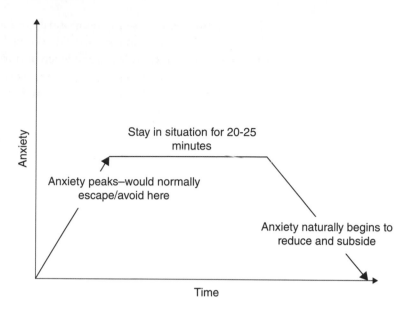

This is a more challenging experience as escaping to check something/ avoidance provides us with immediate and rapid relief from our OCD symptoms, whereas staying in the situation means tolerating the anxiety for 20-25 minutes before it starts to subside. However, by staying in the experience we discover that we can handle difficult and anxiety-provoking situations without having to escape/check/avoid, and this means we can do so much more than if we were constantly trying to escape.

Also, it's wonderful for your confidence and self-esteem to discover you can cope with a situation that you previously thought you couldn't.

⏱ *Exercise 26*

Next time you experience an urge to check/seek reassurance/complete an OCD ritual, try to sit out the situation without acting on the impulse for 25 minutes or so. Try to distract yourself in the meantime. You may find that the urge has reduced enough that you can ignore it and carry on. Even if you do still have to go and check/escape after 25 minutes, you are still loosening the grip of the OCD. You are breaking the cycle of OCD telling you to do something and you *immediately* responding.

By putting in a time delay or 'buffer' you are allowing yourself to learn to tolerate the anxiety for long enough to complete a task/finish a conversation, etc. before responding. This in turn will allow you to do more, in spite of having OCD. Don't forget to log your experiences in your therapy notebook so that you can monitor progress.

→ Challenge the inflated responsibility: are you really responsible for this?

We mentioned previously how inflated responsibility is a common problem in OCD. In order to address this we need to consider what we are *actually* responsible for, rather than just accepting 100 per cent responsibility. It is important to consider responsibility carefully and make sure we are not carrying the responsibility of others, as the greater the feeling of responsibility, the greater the OCD symptoms.

To make sure we only carry our responsibility and no one else's, we can use a pie chart to divide up our responsibility. Let's look at an example:

Case study: Sandra

Sandra asks her husband to pop out and grab some milk while she makes the children's dinner. Her husband seems to be gone longer than Sandra anticipated and she suddenly has an intrusive image of something being wrong with the car and her husband having an accident. Sandra begins to feel absolutely awful and feels 100 per cent responsibility, thinking to herself: 'If only I hadn't asked him to go then nothing would have happened – it's all my fault.'

If we were to draw out how Sandra views her responsibility in this situation it would look like this:

My responsibility

However, let's think about Sandra's situation more realistically. Sandra's only responsible for asking her husband to go. However, if something had happened then her own responsibility would be very small. Immediately we need to consider the responsibility of her husband and other road users, the car manufacturer, not to mention other elements such as the weather. So realistically Sandra's pie chart looks more like this:

Responsibility

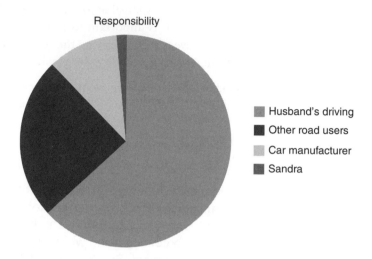

- Husband's driving
- Other road users
- Car manufacturer
- Sandra

Sandra does still have some responsibility but only a tiny amount compared to what she originally thought. It isn't realistic to think that we hold responsibility for absolutely everything – we need to gain a more realistic picture of our own responsibilities.

🕐 *Exercise 27*

Think of some situations that you currently feel *completely* responsible for. Now evaluate them honestly and think how you can divide that responsibility. Use the empty pie chart below to help you plot your responsibility and other people's. If you struggle to do this then ask someone else for their opinion, since an objective outsider may be better at seeing a more realistic picture.

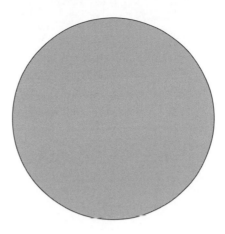

By re-evaluating your responsibility you can let go of feeling 100 per cent responsible at all times. If you can reduce your feeling of responsibility, then you can also reduce your anxiety accordingly.

Key points from this chapter

- ▶ There are many different strategies we can use to challenge our OCD thinking and behaviours.

- ▶ By seeking evidence we are able to challenge our thoughts and our behaviours.

- ▶ Evidence needs to be actual evidence – thoughts and anxieties do not count since *thoughts are just thoughts* not facts.

- ▶ Behavioural experiments allow us to gather evidence to challenge our thoughts and our behaviours, and are a practical way of doing so.

- ▶ Make sure your behavioural experiment tests a specific idea and feels challenging but do able, then go for it!

Where to next?

This chapter has focused on a variety of techniques for overcoming your OCD thinking and behaviours. The next chapter examines another OCD-related behaviour, which is reassurance seeking, and looks at ways of challenging and overcoming our need to seek reassurance.

⑨ Reassurance

About this chapter

▶ Seeking reassurance from others is one of the major components of OCD and can act as a strong maintaining factor. This chapter will therefore discuss the ways in which we might seek reassurance, how reassurance works (or doesn't) and how to break the habit of reassurance-seeking and replace it with something more helpful. This chapter will be helpful for both those with OCD, and those being asked to offer the reassurance. The issue of reassurance is also touched upon in the chapter for friends, family and carers (FFC).

→ The truth about reassurance

One of the hardest conversations I have with people with OCD is explaining to them that reassurance doesn't work. The reason this is so difficult is because often people's entire days, indeed their entire lives, will be made up of various rituals and behaviours all designed to seek reassurance and alleviate some anxiety. The idea that giving reassurance doesn't work is also challenging for those living with someone with OCD. Having to constantly give reassurance is just one of the ways in which OCD significantly impacts on the lives of those around someone with OCD.

Learning that this might have been 'pointless' is hard to hear and I appreciate how difficult this chapter might be. However, by learning more about reassurance, the way it works and the impact on OCD, you will learn how to overcome this and move on from reassurance (seeking and giving) and there will be lots of tips and help for FFC throughout this chapter.

→ What is reassurance?

So what do we actually mean when we talk about reassurance? Reassurance can take various forms and we may find that we engage in much reassurance-seeking behaviour without even realizing it.

Exercise 28

Look at the table below, which lists different types of reassurance, and place a tick (✓) next to any that apply to you. It may also be good to read this through with any FFC as they may identify reassurance-seeking behaviours that you exhibit that are now so habitual you don't realize that you are doing them.

Type of reassurance seeking	Explanation of this reassurance	Yep, this sounds like me (✓)
Checking	When we check something we are looking to confirm something in our minds, or silence a doubt that has crept in. For example, if I am driving away from my house I may suddenly get an intrusive doubt that makes me question 'did I lock the door?'. Even if we feel quite certain that we did, sometimes that doubt can lead to strong anxiety and so to alleviate, or prevent, that anxiety we may drive back home and 'check' the door is locked. It is not uncommon for people to repeatedly check things around them, even though they know they've already done something/locked something/turned something off.	
Replaying conversations and/or images in our minds	Replaying conversations and/or images is another form of reassurance seeking. We may have a pleasant conversation with someone at work and then as we walk away we may have a doubt 'did I come across as rude?' and this may lead us to worry and so we start to replay the conversation in our head over and over again until we feel reassured that all is well and we didn't offend anyone.	

Scanning the news/ Internet	Now that technology is so readily available, this is a form of reassurance seeking that is increasingly common and can consume hours of someone with OCD's day. This type of reassurance-seeking may happen in response to various different worries but the result is always to try to silence a doubt or anxiety that we have in our minds. For example, if I worry that I am coming down with an illness, I might spend a long time online looking up my symptoms, seeking reassurance that it isn't anything serious. If I believe that I may have accidentally harmed someone without realizing, I may spend hours scanning news websites to see if there have been any reports in my area.	
Checking with a professional/ authority figure	This reassurance seeking involves asking someone who you believe to be an 'authority' on a subject. For example you may visit your GP for reassurance that you are healthy. You may contact a priest to seek reassurance that God isn't angry with you. You may speak to a psychologist to check that this is really OCD and not something else. It is common for people with OCD to start to doubt their own ability in decision-making/ judgement and as such we turn to others who we consider to be 'authorities' for reassurance.	
Involving others	As well as speaking to those we consider an 'authority', it is very common for those with OCD to seek reassurance from those around them in everyday life. For example, you may ask your partner, colleague or friend to reassure you about a conversation you had. Similarly, you may actually ask your FFC to check something for you. This is usually to avoid the anxiety and doubt that you will feel if you have to start checking something yourself. For example, saying to a partner 'please can you check I locked the front door'.	

→ Why does reassurance matter?

The reason why reassurance and reassurance-seeking matter so much in the treatment of OCD is that *seeking and gaining reassurance can actually fuel the OCD and make the OCD stronger*. This can be difficult to understand because reassurance can appear to work, in the short term at least. I work with many FFC who tell me that if they didn't offer reassurance then their partner/friend with OCD would never leave the house. Often that reassurance that everything is ok is enough for someone to be able to get to work or function on a day-to-day basis. In this sense, the reassurance is helpful and I am not criticizing those who need to seek or offer reassurance. However the problem with reassurance is the impact it has in the long term.

The gains and short-term relief from anxiety are indeed short-lived and long-term reassurance seeking and giving is problematic for those seeking to be free from OCD. This will be explained in more detail later in this chapter. For now, let's look at a case study to understand some of the problems that reassurance seeking can cause, and some of the complications that it can bring.

Case study: Kate

Kate started becoming anxious about home security after a leaflet was pushed through her door asking for neighbours to get together and form a neighbourhood watch committee. Kate had never before questioned her neighbourhood, but her OCD-thinking meant that she was now feeling extremely insecure and worried about her neighbourhood. After all, she thought, if the area was safe then they wouldn't need a neighbourhood watch committee.

Kate then started to double-check her front door was locked. At first this wasn't problematic but Kate then began to worry about the house being watched and so she made a great show of checking her windows and doors and pulling curtains, etc. Kate lived alone but, after becoming fearful that her house was being watched, she started to shout 'Bye darling – see you later!' when she left in the morning.

Kate found that she couldn't stop these behaviours, even when quite embarrassingly her neighbours caught her shouting to her imaginary guest. Kate explained her fears to her neighbour, who said the area was very safe and that there hadn't been any problems before. Kate asked the neighbour if she wouldn't mind checking on the house when she was out at work all day. The neighbour agreed and so Kate started to go to work more happily.

While at work Kate found that she couldn't stop worrying about her house and so she called her neighbour, who said that everything was fine. Kate then called her neighbour again who reassured her again, but Kate thought she heard some suspicious background noise. Kate called again later in the day and her neighbour answered the phone sounding annoyed and she said,

'I've already told you your house is fine – please stop calling me!' and hung up. Kate then began to worry that because her neighbour was annoyed with her then she would deliberately ignore any suspicious signs/noises and would not protect Kate's home.

Kate became unbearably anxious and eventually went and told her boss she felt unwell and had to go home. Kate arrived home and went round to her neighbour's house to apologize. Her neighbour relented and said 'it's ok … it's understandable really' as she closed the door. Kate's mind then immediately started to replay those words and wonder what her neighbour meant by 'understandable' – was this because she also believed it was a dangerous neighbourhood? After all, if it were really safe then the neighbour wouldn't have agreed to watch the house, would she?

The above case study offers an insight into how someone with OCD thinks. How something as seemingly innocent as a leaflet pushed through the door can become a trigger for OCD thinking. We have already addressed how to challenge this OCD thinking earlier in this workbook, so let's focus on the problematic elements of reassurance seeking.

→ What's the problem?

1 Kate is seeking reassurance for a problem that she doesn't actually have any evidence for, i.e. the idea that her neighbourhood is dangerous and her house will be targeted by criminals. Her house has not been broken into nor has she seen anyone watching her house, yet she is indulging in these out-of-character, time-consuming and occasionally embarrassing behaviours based on this belief about her 'dangerous' neighbourhood.

2 Kate is giving all the responsibility for her home's welfare to a neighbour, who agrees to check the house for her. In agreeing to this, the neighbour is accidentally confirming Kate's belief that the neighbourhood is dangerous, and that her house needs watching. This confirmation serves as 'proof' for the OCD thinking and maintains the OCD ideas.

3 Kate then continually seeks reassurance, which begins to irritate her neighbour.

4 Her neighbour, in trying to be helpful and kind, says something that then makes Kate believe her home is in danger after all.

As you can see from the above, seeking and giving reassurance is problematic because it can serve to *confirm* rather than discredit unhelpful OCD thoughts. When people seek reassurance they often know the reassurance they need from someone else, but often the person being asked to reassure doesn't know what is needed/wanted. This makes it very easy for someone to say the 'wrong' thing and this can lead to further OCD beliefs as well as cause difficulties and misunderstandings in relationships with others.

Let's consider the alternative scenario. Had Kate's neighbour said 'I'm not watching the house', then Kate would have been unable to seek reassurance in that form. Then when nothing bad happened Kate would have seen that she didn't need to go to such extreme measures to keep her home secure as it wasn't at risk.

The reassurance from the neighbour was offering Kate some hope that she could be *certain* that her home is secure, which is near impossible. Life simply does not work in these certainties. It would be far better for Kate to learn that she doesn't *need* certainty and to let go of the anxiety, accepting that some things are out of her control. As much as we would like 100 per cent certainty we cannot obtain it and seeking it only leads to *increased* anxiety. Kate's reassurance seeking is maintaining her OCD-driven thoughts and beliefs and reinforcing her need for certainty.

Exercise 29

Consider the ideas above and then turn your attention to your own situation. Think of a time when you recently sought reassurance. If you are reading this book for someone else then think back to the last time they asked you for reassurance. Now think of any problems that this reassurance seeking or giving caused you and think about how this might have sustained an OCD thought/belief in the long term.

Write down your experiences using the headings below:

Last time I sought/was asked to give reassurance

_____

_____

_____

_____

_____

_____

_____

_____

Did it seem to work?

_____

_____

_____

_____

_____

_____

_____

Did it completely remove the thought/belief forever?

_____

_____

_____

_____

_____

_____

_____

_____

_____

Did I ask/was I asked more than once?

_____

_____

_____

_____

_____

_____

Did this cause a problem in the relationship? E.g. were you/they annoyed or irritated by constantly offering reassurance?

_____

_____

_____

_____

_____

_____

_____

→ Reassurance feeds the OCD

What we can see from the above is that reassurance does in fact 'feed' the OCD. It makes the OCD thoughts and beliefs stronger and harder to shift. Also, after a while OCD introduces doubt so that even once reassurance is given, the person with OCD may continue to seek reassurance, as new doubts or worries will come to mind.

I AM SEEKING REASSURANCE CONSTANTLY. HOW DO I STOP?

Seeking reassurance can become such an ingrained habit that we may seek reassurance in lots and so many different ways we scarcely any longer even notice.

🕐 *Exercise 30*

Take a moment to write down some of the many things you seek reassurance about and start to think about the impact:

_____

_____

_____

_____

_____

_____

_____

_____

_____

_____

_____

_____

_____

_____

_____

When we think about giving up reassurance seeking it can feel very scary since OCD can take away all our confidence and make us feel incapable of managing a situation without constant reassurance. Try using some of the tips below to help you break the habit.

1 *Stop and think*. Instead of automatically checking or questioning something, stop and give yourself a breather. OCD wants us to check or ask for reassurance immediately. Although it may feel scary at first, try to resist the temptation for at least 25 minutes to allow the anxiety to fade (as discussed earlier).

Set a timer and distract yourself in the meantime by doing something else. Then once the timer goes off only check/seek reassurance if you still feel you really need to, and even then only ask once. Gradually increase the length of time before you seek reassurance/check and you may find that with distractions and the reduction of the anxiety the compulsion fades by itself.

2 *Challenge the thought/belief that is behind the need for reassurance.* For example, if you don't believe you have turned the cooker off correctly, stop and think what is behind that belief. Perhaps it is a fear of burning the house down? If so, stop and challenge that belief – run through some questions in your mind to challenge the belief. For example:

a Have I ever done it before?

b Am I likely to do it?

c Is this common?

d Do I read about it in the newspapers/hear it on the news every day?

e If not, then is it much more likely that this is an extremely rare and unlikely circumstance?

f Is it possible that this is just OCD?

g Had OCD just told you that it's not OCD?

3 *Once is enough*. Set yourself a new rule. I always say to patients that 'if you ask something once then that is seeking new information; if you ask something twice then that is reassurance seeking and I won't answer it'. Set this rule and try it yourself. Ask once for new information and no more – you don't need to seek reassurance, it's OCD that does.

I AM GIVING REASSURANCE CONSTANTLY, WHAT SHOULD I BE DOING INSTEAD?

Often, when I speak to the FFC of those with OCD, they tell me that they are fully aware that reassurance is unhelpful but that they simply don't know what to do instead. Try to follow some of the tips in the 'breaking out from reassurance giving' guide below:

Breaking out from reassurance giving:

1 *Explain*: Explain why you are going to be stopping the reassurance.

   It is unrealistic to expect the person with OCD to know that you will suddenly stop reassuring them and they may find the prospect extremely frightening, so it is important to explain to them that reassurance simply maintains the cycle of OCD and that it is actually making them worse in the long term. Explain that stopping reassurance is part of helping someone to overcome their OCD.

2 *Ration*: If stopping suddenly feels unmanageable then start to ration out your reassurance.

   Tell the person with OCD that you are going to only offer them, for example, three reassurances per day. This will reduce the stress and strain on you, and will force the person with OCD to stop seeking reassurance as habit and consider when they really do need reassurance. You can also start higher and start to wean off reassurance, so that you are offering less and less until you no longer have to offer reassurance.

3 *Remember it's the OCD*: This is very important.

   You are not helping the person with OCD but instead are helping the OCD itself when you offer reassurance. It is the OCD that is seeking reassurance, and it is the OCD that is appeased when you comply. Remember, to help the person you care about you need to stop interacting with the OCD.

4 *Encourage them to try*: If you find that the person with OCD seeks reassurance by asking you to do/check things for them, encourage them to try first while offering your support.

   By showing that you trust them to check the cooker is off, for example, they will begin to rebuild their confidence and know that they can cope. OCD introduces such a terrible doubt that people quickly lose their faith in their own ability.

   Think of how we teach children; if we rush in at every step then they do not learn and develop and instead become completely adult-dependent and cannot be independent. The same is true with OCD. It is only by allowing someone to try, and letting them know that you are supporting and trusting their attempt, that individuals with OCD will rebuild their confidence and learn to trust themselves again.

By using the strategies above you will be able to break out of the cycle of reassurance giving, and be able to help the person with OCD move away from needing so much reassurance.

Key points from this chapter

- ► Seeking and gaining reassurance can actually fuel the OCD and make the OCD stronger
- ► After a while OCD introduces doubt so that even once reassurance is given, the person with OCD may continue to seek reassurance, as new doubts or worries will come to mind
- ► When reassuring you are not helping the person with OCD but instead are helping the OCD itself.

Where to next?

In the next chapter we move on to look at the issue of perfectionism and the problem of perfectionist behaviours. There will be exercises to complete to help you to identify and overcome any problematic perfectionist tendencies and behaviours.

10 Perfectionism

▶ You may be wondering why a chapter on perfectionism is being included in a book about OCD. The reality is that it is common for those affected by OCD to experience perfectionist tendencies. While some of these tendencies can be motivating and helpful, perfectionism itself can be damaging and affect one's ability to work, rest and socialize.

▶ Perfectionism can also be detrimental to self-esteem and ruin self-confidence. Therefore this is an important topic to be mindful of and be aware of as part of your journey to overcoming OCD.

→ Wait, I'm confused ... isn't perfection a *good* thing?

The term 'perfect' is often used in everyday language to describe something wonderful or as a compliment. For example, if someone said to you 'wow this cake you baked is perfect!' you'd be pretty pleased with that compliment. The word 'perfect' implies that there is no room for improvement. Perfect means that there is absolutely no way that it could be improved upon and if you worked on something tirelessly for another ten years you still wouldn't improve it. Pretty impressive, huh?

So why is perfectionism a problem? The problem comes when people aim to achieve this 'perfect' standard in absolutely everything they do. For example, they may not be able to cope if they make a mistake and may experience huge anxiety and self-reproach if they do.

This is where the OCD tendencies can become evident. While someone is trying to protect themselves from the fear and anxiety generated by perfectionism, they may engage in a series of checking and reassurance seeking rituals. These rituals may overtake the original task and prevent them from achieving what they want to achieve/need to get done in a day.

Read through the case study below and, as you do so, highlight or make some notes on what problems Emily's perfectionism is causing her:

Case study: Emily

Emily works as an admin assistant in a marketing firm. She has been in her job for seven years and is responsible for the team admin. Emily has always liked going to work but over the past few years she has felt that her workload has become increasingly unmanageable.

Emily believes that things should always be done to the highest standard possible and prides herself on her work. Emily always used to get compliments on her 'perfect' PowerPoint skills and her 'perfect' filing system. Lately, however, Emily is struggling. Her 'perfect' filing system takes time and as she does not have the time to do it properly, she is leaving filing on her desk until she has time to complete the task to her own high standard. Emily's colleague Michelle has offered to help but Emily doesn't think Michelle will do the filing as well as she would. Emily feels if someone else helps she would lose track of things and wouldn't be able to check that they were done 'properly'. Therefore Emily has refused the offer of help.

Meanwhile, the pile on her desk grows bigger every day and Emily now feels totally overwhelmed by the task in front of her. Emily has also noticed that some of the team are being short with her. They have accused her of losing invoices and other important bits of paper. Emily knows they are not lost, they are in the pile on her desk but she doesn't want to move anything or else the order for filing will be wrong. The team are becoming frustrated but Emily doesn't understand why they are criticizing her for wanting to do things properly.

Emily is also angry and confused by a recent rumour that Michelle is going to be promoted to admin manager, meaning she'd be Emily's boss. Michelle has only been at the company for two years and Emily feels that her own standards are higher than Michelle's and that it should be her being promoted instead.

Hearing this rumour has made Emily even more determined to do things 'properly' and show her value. As such, she is spending a long time checking and re-checking her emails, reports and files for errors. Often Emily feels very anxious after something is sent and worries that she has made a mistake or not phrased something well and will have caused some offence. Emily then becomes very anxious that she will be seen as useless and will be sacked. Emily has started to check with people after sending an email that they were happy with it, often unable to stop herself interrupting them and asking them to read the email there and then, or sending several follow-up emails, checking that she hasn't offended anyone or made a mistake.

Recently, people have become frustrated by Emily's slow progress at work and have been snappy and short with her. Emily is now more determined than ever to make things 'right' and to prove her worth and so she is working longer and longer hours and even when no one is there late at night in order to complete her filing and get on with things. Unfortunately, progress is slow and Emily doesn't know how she will ever get everything completed. Emily is feeling lonely and depressed at work, and she no longer feels any job satisfaction.

So why is Emily's perfectionism a problem?

Poor old Emily! She is not having an easy time of it. Her high standards are leading to slow progress and minimal achievement. She is mistrusting of others meaning she won't accept help with her work and is having to do it all herself. She is overwhelmed by her workload and her colleagues are getting short with her. She no longer enjoys work and now a seeming 'junior' colleague is being promoted ahead of her. This is definitely not a 'perfect' situation for her. Keep a hold of your notes on this as we'll be coming back to Emily later.

Exercise 31

In order to determine whether your perfectionism is a problem, have a look at the perfectionist statements below and tick 'yes' if it applies to you and 'no' if it doesn't apply to you:

Statement	Yes – this applies to me (✓)	No – this does not apply to me (✓)
I believe there is a right way to do everything		
I should always aim to do everything that I do to the highest standard, no matter how small the task		
Perfection is attainable if you work hard enough		
I am frustrated by other people's 'sloppy' standards		
Sometimes people around me don't appreciate why things are important/why they take me so long		
I spend more time and care on tasks than on other people		
I ask others to try to do things my way or the way I would do them e.g. housework		
I often have to redo others' work as it is not to a high enough standard		
I never seem to have enough time to do things		
Sometimes my high standards leave me exhausted		

Mainly 'Yes's:

If you have ticked mainly 'yes' in response to these questions, then it is likely that you hold problematic perfectionist beliefs. This chapter will teach you techniques to overcome problematic perfectionism.

Mainly 'No's:

If you have ticked mainly 'no' in response to these questions and you are not distressed or unable to achieve what you want to due to your perfectionism, then it probably isn't presenting a problem. It may still be interesting to read through the techniques designed to prevent perfectionism from becoming a problem, in case they are helpful for future reference.

→ If I'm not doing things perfectly then what's the point?

Now there's a statement of black-and-white thinking if ever I heard one! It's common for people with perfectionism to assume that if something isn't done properly then it's shoddy or of a poor standard and therefore not worth doing. However, we need to remember that we can still strive for 'excellent' and 'outstanding' results within our work. Overcoming perfectionism is not about ditching high standards, it's about letting go of an unrealistic notion that something can be 'perfect'.

→ Want to know a secret? 'Perfect' doesn't exist!

If you read the above statement and gasped in shock or immediately disagreed then you are not alone. Many people struggle with the idea that there is no such thing as 'perfect'. Hear me out though. The idea of 'perfect' is a subjective and socially constructed idea. What I mean by that is that your version of 'perfect' and someone else's idea of 'perfect' may look completely different. If you think I'm wrong then try asking a group of ten women what makes a perfect mother. I can guarantee you that they will all have very different ideas about what makes the 'perfect' mother and yet they are all using the same standard of 'perfection'.

So you see, 'perfect' as an outside, tangible, objective idea *simply does not exist*. We have to make the rules ourselves, deciding what makes something or someone 'perfect'. The reason this becomes problematic is because 'perfectionism' is a sneaky creature and often shifts the goalposts.

Let's go back to that delicious cake you baked. You may set it down on the table and people gasp in delight and say 'wow that's perfect'. Immediately a voice in your head will say 'well it would be perfect if the icing hadn't smudged slightly there' or 'well maybe if it was a little bit more flavoured', 'maybe next time I should make it a tiny bit bigger', and so on. All of these thoughts are perfectionist thoughts. Perfectionist thoughts could also be re-named as 'fault finders', and they go over things we've done or said and find fault in it. This may seem motivating as it's something that drives us on to better things but let's just reconsider the CBT model here.

Situation

Thoughts

Behaviour

Feelings

Physical symptoms

If our thoughts, feelings, behaviours and physical symptoms are all linked, then you can see how constantly finding fault with everything you do is going to quickly lead to you feeling useless, incompetent, overwhelmed and exhausted. It is very common for those with perfectionism to avoid starting tasks because the sheer exhaustion of having to complete them to a high standard feels overwhelming. Also, being unable to meet these perfectionist standards often results in high anxiety, loss of self-esteem and diminished job satisfaction.

Let's go back to Emily. Let's quickly recap on why Emily's perfectionism was causing her problems.

▶ She was unable to complete tasks
▶ She was feeling overwhelmed
▶ She was disrupting colleagues

- ▶ She was irritating others
- ▶ She was being overlooked for promotion
- ▶ She was working longer and longer hours for a job that should have been quick and standard in her role
- ▶ She was not accepting help from others
- ▶ She was working to an unrealistic and self-imposed standard.

Consider the last point here – this is often where the problem lies in perfectionism. The very high and problematic standards have often been created by ourselves; they are not being expected of us by anyone else. While Emily is fretting over every tiny detail and wants everything to be perfect, her colleagues are frustrated by how slow her work is and simply want things organized and done so they can track their paperwork. Emily is not fulfilling her job role and won't accept help from others because she thinks her way is the right way. However, from the outside perspective, no one has asked Emily to do things 'perfectly'.

Driving Emily's perfectionist behaviour is a high anxiety and the belief that unless everything is perfect she will be considered useless and be sacked. Ironically, if Emily doesn't stop trying to do things 'perfectly' and get on with things then she's likely to be sacked anyway!

⏰ Exercise 32

It is important to work through your perfectionist behaviours and consider the underlying beliefs that are driving them. (Tip: think back to the work on digging deeper and uncovering deeper beliefs.)

Now consider some of your own perfectionist behaviours. List them below:

_____

_____

_____

_____

_____

_____

_____

_____

_____

_____

_____

_____

_____

_____

_____

_____

_____

_____

Ask yourself, what would happen if you didn't complete these behaviours/work in this way? Write your answer below:

_____

_____

_____

_____

_____

_____

_____

_____

_____

_____

Now consider your answer above. Can you recognize any thinking errors? Is there any evidence to support your belief?

_____

_____

_____

_____

_____

_____

_____

_____

Now also consider what you think it would say about you as a person if you didn't act in this way/carry out these perfectionist behaviours. Write your answer below:

_____

_____

_____

_____

_____

_____

_____

_____

_____

_____

_____

_____

_____

_____

_____

_____

Thinking about these beliefs, again look for evidence for them –
are they realistic? Is there any evidence to support this? Are you
experiencing thinking errors? Is the problem the behaviour itself or
is it the thinking and beliefs underneath that is causing the problem?

Consider now what impact this is having on you and your mood.
Write your observations below:

_____

_____

_____

_____

_____

_____

_____

_____

_____

_____

_____

_____

_____

_____

_____

_____

_____

_____

Is there a downside to this? Are your perfectionist behaviours affecting your mood? Would you feel happier without these behaviours?

_____

_____

_____

_____

_____

_____

_____

_____

_____

→ A realistic picture ...

Remember, what Emily's company actually wanted was for her to complete her job. Her company would have happily settled for 'good enough' e.g. working to a good-enough standard to fulfil her role and meet the team's needs. That was all.

However, Emily was holding an unhelpful belief that she had generated for herself and was working to that subjective idea of 'perfect', as opposed to the real-world view of 'good enough'. In order to change this Emily needed to recognize the difference between being 'perfect' and achieving high standards.

→ Breaking the perfectionist barrier

The first step in overcoming your perfectionist tendencies is to accept that perfect does not exist. This is a tough, yet very necessary, part of overcoming perfectionism. While people can be excellent, high achieving and wildly successful at work, they cannot be the 'perfect' employee, because 'perfect' is not an objective term. Therefore, what one person considers perfect may not be the same as for another person.

Try to get your head around this idea first before doing anything else. Recognize that perfectionism is simply in the same anxiety family as OCD. Perfectionism makes you do things or check things in a certain way. It makes you rigid and inflexible and unable to operate in any way other than to the strict rules that perfectionism gives you.

In order to explore this idea further, look for examples of the idea that perfect doesn't exist in the real world. Is there such a thing as a 'perfect' body? Would everyone agree on this? Ask others around you what they think. Do you disagree on something? Do you have different versions of perfect?

Second, consider the pros and cons of perfect versus good enough. Again use Emily's example as a guide. Emily's 'perfect' behaviour meant she was failing at work, was unable to complete anything, was annoying her colleagues, being overlooked for promotion and got no job satisfaction. Had Emily let go of her 'perfect' ideas and just worked to a 'good enough' standard then she would have been on top of her work, a more likely candidate for promotion, able to share her workload and accept help from others, less irritating and more flexible to work with. Not to mention all the positive impact on Emily's mood and energy.

Exercise 33

The pros of letting go of 'perfect' ideas are endless. Write your own pros and cons list below, using your own perfectionism. Be sure to look for any evidence for the 'cons' as they tend to be based on anxiety rather than fact.

Perfectionist idea/behaviour	Pros of letting this go	Cons of letting this go

Third, challenge the ideas behind your perfectionism. Once you identify the ideas that are driving your perfectionist behaviours, challenge them. Use a series of thought challenges and behavioural experiments as discussed in previous chapters to help you question and challenge some of the ideas.

Next, define 'good enough'. It can be tricky to learn where to draw the line on good enough versus 'perfect'. Other people can help. If you are worried about falling below certain standards at work then arrange a meeting with your line manager and express your concerns and ask them what it is they expect from you.

Work with others to draw up a list of expectations and make sure you are confident in what you are being asked to do. Equally at home, if you worry about being a good enough partner/spouse/child/parent, and so on, then discuss these ideas with others and get a wider perspective. You need to move away from the self-imposed ideas of 'perfect' and embrace a wider held view so that you know what you are aiming for.

Finally, if you're not sure then try it! If you don't think 'good enough' will work for you then that's just a thought and not actual evidence, so try it. Set yourself a challenge and for a month drop those perfectionist tendencies and do things to a 'good enough' standard. Monitor and record all your progress and successes and then at the end of the month review this progress and ask yourself whether you got more done and achieved more aiming for good enough versus perfect. Are you happier? Are you more relaxed and less exhausted? If there is any residual anxiety left over then discover what is beneath it and challenge it.

All of the techniques discussed in this chapter will be familiar by now; these are the ways that we overcome all anxiety, including OCD and perfectionism. But beware of sabotaging yourself. Perfectionism is often determined to make us fail and pick holes in what we do. Recognize that as just another trick of anxiety, *it is not fact*.

Using the techniques discussed will help you identify, challenge and move away from destructive 'perfectionist' beliefs and behaviours and will allow you to develop the true confidence that comes from knowing that you are truly good enough, without the need to be 'perfect'.

Key points to remember

▶ There is no such thing as perfect. The notion of 'perfect' is a subjective idea and it doesn't actually exist.

▶ Letting go of perfectionism is not the same as dropping high standards. You can strive for excellence without the anxiety and distress that can come from striving for perfection.

▶ Why do things need to be perfect anyway? Remember to question and challenge where your notion of needing to be perfect came from.

▶ It is important to uncover and challenge the thoughts and beliefs that are maintaining your perfectionism.

▶ If you think 'good enough' won't work for you then set a target and try it for a month and see how you go. Don't dismiss it without trying it and gaining evidence about whether or not it works for you.

Where to next?

This chapter has focused on perfectionism and taught you some techniques to help you overcome some of your anxiety-provoking ideas and behaviours. The next chapter is aimed at friends, family members and carers (FFC) and is designed to help them understand OCD more generally, and to learn strategies and techniques to support your journey in overcoming your own OCD.

Friends, Family and Carers (FFC) – how do we help?

About this chapter

▶ This chapter is for friends, family and carers (FFC), that is, those around the person with the diagnosis. This is particularly important because OCD can impact on and affect everyone, not just the person who has the OCD.

▶ OCD has a way of drawing in and requiring support and help from other people, and, if this is you, it is important that you receive some guidance and support through your own experiences. There may be ideas and strategies that you can implement yourself to support someone's journey out of OCD.

▶ This chapter is designed to offer you some information, help and support for dealing with someone else's OCD. There is also an emphasis on looking after you, which may feel counter intuitive but which will be explained fully. This chapter should provide you with an understanding of what OCD is; how it may be affecting the person you know, and you; how best to deal with OCD; and how to change your own behaviour to support them.

▶ This chapter will also discuss some of the potential impacts of being around/living with someone with a diagnosis of OCD; what you can do to help; and how to manage some of your own emotions around/reactions to the OCD.

→ Living with OCD

Often in therapy the focus will, quite rightly, be on the person with the OCD diagnosis. However, the person with the diagnosis is not the only person affected by the OCD, they are generally just the only one getting any help and support.

As you may have seen earlier in the book, I describe OCD as a separate person. This means that if you live with someone with OCD, you are also living with an unwelcome and uninvited stranger. This stranger takes over your lives, changes the way your household runs, dictates what you can and can't do and often affects very personal elements of our relationships such as our sex life or other intimacy. So it's important to understand who this OCD stranger is, how they are affecting you, and how you can help kick them out of your friendship/relationship. Remember, OCD was not invited into the situation, it barged in and there are lots of things that you can do in order to show it the door!

→ I'm not the one with OCD. It doesn't really affect me. If they're ok then I'm ok

I often hear this from partners and close friends of those with OCD and it's important to recognize that OCD is clever and manipulative and may have got you involved in someone else's OCD without you even realizing.

For example, do any of the below situations look familiar to you?

▶ I have taken over some day-to-day tasks in order to reduce my partner/friend's anxiety.

▶ I have taken over responsibility for certain areas in our shared life e.g. bills/finances, childcare, correspondence, cleaning.

▶ I often have to offer reassurance and let them know that I am ok/that a situation is safe or resolved etc.

▶ I now do things and think about things that I never used to.

▶ Some of my behaviour could be seen as extreme e.g. made to strip at the door before entering house for fear of bringing in germs, made to wear gloves when touching things, not allowed to feed children certain foods for fear of poisoning them.

- My partner or friend repeats things that I have already done e.g. checks a letter I have already checked, hoovers a room I have already hovered.
- I find at least an hour of my day is spent reassuring them or acting in a way that is designed to alleviate their anxiety.
- I am no longer spontaneous.
- I don't do things with them as much as I'd like e.g. go out for dinner/ cinema because of their OCD and the way it makes them feel.

If you have recognized one or more of the above statements then you are indeed being affected by someone else's OCD. Living with/being around someone with an anxiety disorder can be challenging, not least because we often don't know how to help.

Also, being around someone who is constantly anxious can leave us feeling uncertain of their mood and this uncertainty can be exhausting, make it hard to make plans and difficult to know what will happen next.

→ They are no longer the person I met/used to know

When I describe OCD to people, I talk about a big chaotic messy bully. This bully often stands between you and the person you are familiar with, almost hiding them to a point where you can only see the bully and not the person that you know and care about. It can be very difficult to see the person as you knew them; instead you are faced with a highly anxious, worried and sometimes incredibly demanding person to be with. It is important to remember that although they appear to have changed it is the OCD that you are seeing, not the person underneath. This is important because once the OCD is dealt with, it then means that you can help that person remember who they were and to move forward to who they want to be.

→ It is important to recognize and discuss your own reaction to the OCD

OCD can make people highly anxious and this anxiety can seem to completely engulf the person you know and replace them with a nervous wreck who cannot stop worrying. This can be distressing for many reasons, not least because anxiety is unpleasant and watching someone you care about experience anxiety is very difficult. OCD can get in the way of social occasions and/or work, which can place a strain on a friendship or relationship, and make situations difficult for you.

Start to separate out these experiences from the person you care about. Start to notice when the person is present versus when OCD is present.

People talk about how their marriage or partnership/ friendship has become crowded by the anxiety and that's because it is as though a third and very unwelcome person has moved into your household. This unwelcome visitor is OCD and it can seem to dominate everything. However do not worry. OCD is not a permanent house guest and you can help kick it out of your household, no matter how strong it feels at times.

→ Blame the OCD – not the person who has it

When you are reflecting and commenting on how the OCD has changed someone, it is really important to pin the blame on the OCD and not the person. After all, they are not choosing to feel like this and so it is important that they don't feel they are being 'blamed' for their anxiety.

For example, if OCD has made someone struggle to make decisions it is important to say 'your OCD seems to have made it really difficult to make any decisions' rather than 'you can't make any decisions at the moment'. This seems a subtle difference but it is important that you reinforce the ideas in this book that describe OCD as something a person has rather than who they are.

To look at this a different way, imagine if the person you care about had a cold. You wouldn't start blaming them for being snotty and sneezy. Instead you might say 'wow your cold is really bad at the moment' as opposed to accusing them of deliberately sneezing through dinner/a meeting/coffee.

The same applies with OCD. Instead of saying to someone 'Gosh you are such a worrier just calm down!' you could say to them 'Gosh your OCD is really kicking off today – look how anxious it's making you!'. This is still highlighting that there is a problem but it is shifting the blame from the individual to the OCD.

⏱ Exercise 34

Write some of the situations you are experiencing below and practise changing them into statements about OCD instead of being about the person themselves. Once you have a list of behaviours that OCD is to blame for, then this will make it easier to discuss them with the individual without putting the blame on them.

Original statement	Re-worked statement
e.g. You always ask me to check things for you but you don't listen and it drives me nuts!	e.g. The OCD gets you to ask me to check things but then when I do it makes you doubt what I've said. It's really difficult for me and the OCD drives me nuts!

→ **I get so angry/fed up with them and then I feel bad – after all, it's not their fault**

Let's just take a moment to think about the statement above, as this is a very common experience among carers or family members/friends of those dealing with OCD.

 *Exercise 35*

First, it's important to recognize the impact that the OCD is having on you. Have a look at the statements below that relate to the ways anxiety can affect us and interfere in our lives. Looking at the statements, circle the ones that you agree with. There is also space underneath provided to write in your own experiences and examples that may not be listed below:

The ways in which someone else's OCD is interfering in my life:

I don't talk to them as much as I used to

_____

_____

_____

_____

_____

I don't share my problems with them as I don't want to worry them

_____

_____

_____

_____

_____

I take on more responsibility than I used to

_____

_____

_____

_____

_____

I do more than my fair share around the house/at work/with day-to-day tasks because they cannot cope

_____

_____

_____

_____

_____

I have to deal with a lot more e.g. family circumstances and events, life events, illness on my own

_____

_____

_____

_____

_____

I don't feel supported anymore

_____

_____

_____

_____

_____

I feel my role has changed from friend/partner/spouse/colleague to
one of a carer

_____

_____

_____

_____

I'm shouted at a lot more/we have more arguments than we used to

_____

_____

_____

_____

I do more/put up with a lot for an easy life

_____

_____

_____

_____

I don't recognize the person they have become/OCD has changed
them so much

_____

_____

_____

_____

_____

They constantly need reassurance and will interrupt what I am doing in order for me to reassure them e.g. eating, working, sleeping

_____

_____

_____

_____

_____

I find myself worrying about things alone so as not to add to their list of anxieties

_____

_____

_____

_____

_____

I feel I carry more burden than they do as I try not to give them anything else to deal with

_____

_____

_____

_____

_____

When they are feeling anxious they withdraw. It doesn't matter what I am saying or doing, they are not really in the moment with me

_____

_____

_____

_____

_____

I am exhausted by their anxiety

_____

_____

_____

_____

_____

I have to deal with all the finances and bills in our household as they can't

_____

_____

_____

_____

_____

Use the space provided below to write down your own experiences of and reactions to someone else's OCD that may not have been included in the above statements:

_____

_____

_____

Now remove yourself from the situation and imagine a friend is telling you that they have been experiencing some of the above. Wouldn't you think they were entitled to feel angry or fed up? Whether the person can help it or not, being put in these situations is an exhausting, frustrating and distressing process and it is important to recognize that.

Thinking back to the work you did previously where you separated out the person with OCD from the OCD itself, it is important to recognize what OCD is doing in these situations. Therefore it is not the person you are angry at, but rather their OCD. It is not them you are fed up with, but you are fed up with dealing with their OCD.

By separating the two out and recognizing that it is absolutely normal and reasonable to be fed up with that person's OCD, you can get rid of some of the guilt and blame you put on yourself. It is ok to be angry with OCD. Just recognize that it is the OCD that you are angry at and not the person with the OCD. This can also be an important message to share with the person who has OCD, as they will be worried about your reaction and how you are feeling.

I CONSTANTLY TELL THEM THEY HAVE NOTHING TO WORRY ABOUT BUT IT DOESN'T SEEM TO STOP THEM WORRYING. HOW CAN I GET THROUGH TO THEM?

Being asked to reassure someone is a very common experience for those close to someone with OCD. There are many different ways in which we can be asked for, and offer, reassurance, sometimes without even realizing we are reassuring someone.

For example, if you are always the last person to leave the house, this may just be coincidence. However, it may that you are offering some reassurance about the house being locked securely or that everything is turned off. It may not even be that the person with OCD realizes they are doing this, but sometimes it is as though they are giving you the responsibility and then can reassure themselves that if anything goes wrong it is your fault (charming!).

However we offer reassurance, either by answering direct questions or checking something for someone, what you will notice is that the reassurance doesn't work. If reassurance worked then we would never be anxious, and there'd be no need for this book. The reason reassurance doesn't work is because it can actually feed the OCD in lots of different ways.

Although initially the person may feel less anxious, very quickly the anxiety will creep back and their OCD will make them feel increasingly anxious and they will need further reassurance and so on. This is a vicious circle to get caught up in because once you reassure, it is very hard to stop reassuring, as you may well have discovered by now.

→ So why does reassurance matter so much?

To understand more about reassurance seeking and giving, return to Chapter 9, which covers this topic in more detail. This section of the workbook is designed to give you a brief overview and some practical strategies to help.

The process of offering reassurance goes against the principles of CBT therapy, which are about challenging the anxious thoughts and discovering for ourselves what happens when we go through a situation. The case study example below describes a situation involving an anxious child and their parents and highlights the role reassurance played in maintaining the child's anxiety.

Case study: Lucy

Lucy, aged 10, had a bad dream one night that she left her bedroom window open and a ghost slipped through her window and into her parents' room where it killed them both. Following this dream, Lucy became very scared about going to bed and the following night asked her parents to check that both her bedroom windows were closed and that nothing could get through.

Lucy's parents checked the windows for her and offered her the reassurance that the windows were closed and that no baddies or ghosts could get through.

Lucy thought to herself: 'I'm right to worry because if the ghost wasn't real then they wouldn't also be worried about the ghost and wouldn't be checking my window.' Lucy then became worried about the other windows in the house and wouldn't go to bed until she had walked around the house with both of her parents checking that all the windows were closed. When Lucy's parents became frustrated by this, particularly in the warmer weather, Lucy cried and screamed until they had checked the windows with her.

Lucy's parents didn't like seeing her so distressed and it seemed a small task to do, so they continued to check all the windows with Lucy every night before bed. This means that Lucy's parents could not go out for the evening, or if they did, they needed to be back in time to check the windows with Lucy.

Three things are noticeable from the case study above.

First, you can understand why Lucy thinks there is a real threat. After all, if there were nothing to worry about then her parents wouldn't check would they? What Lucy cannot understand is that they are checking to reassure her not because there is a real threat from any ghost.

Second, you can see why Lucy's parents are offering her this reassurance. To witness someone we care about be very distressed is a heart breaking situation and it seems a small task to complete to keep them calm and alleviate some of their anxiety.

Third, we can see just how quickly reassurance seeking grows and can become out of control. You can start off offering a very small reassurance, which quickly and suddenly grows into a time-consuming evening routine. Suddenly the fear of ghosts is not the problem. Instead the problem is the elaborate checking ritual that Lucy and her parents have developed to help reduce some of this anxiety.

This example shows how quickly reassurance seeking can grow and become problematic. But it also highlights how – although it initially appears helpful – it can actually confirm some OCD worries or anxieties, even though that is not our intention. Therefore it is important to know what to do instead of offering reassurance.

So if I'm not reassuring, what do I do instead?

Help the person to challenge those fears and anxiety-driven beliefs. Had Lucy been in therapy then what Lucy's parents would have been doing is flinging her bedroom windows wide open and then going to bed. That way, in the morning, when they hadn't been killed, Lucy would have realized that there was nothing to worry about. Even though those initial few nights would have been scary for Lucy, very quickly she would have become confident that there was no threat to her parents.

Also, Lucy would have seen that her parents were not concerned at all, and this may have given her some confidence to begin to doubt her anxious beliefs. Equally, when Lucy had the anxiety about the ghost she had dreamed of, she would have had real evidence to counter this anxious belief, which would have dramatically reduced the impact until she stopped having the anxiety altogether.

Therefore, within CBT we are not trying to offer specific reassurance. Instead we are trying to give the person an opportunity to challenge these thoughts. This is a very different approach and one that quashes OCD beliefs once and for all.

If I don't reassure them then they become angry and we argue

OCD can make us behave irrationally and we can snap and shout at people, even if we are very close to them and care about them. Ask yourself 'would I put up with this if the OCD weren't an issue?'. If the answer is 'no', then don't tolerate the behaviour. Instead, have a conversation explaining how this is making you feel and explain that even though you know it's the OCD, that doesn't mean you have to put up with this behaviour.

Using evidence and support instead of reassurance

As discussed in previous chapters throughout this workbook, the best way to overcome OCD is to challenge and gain evidence against the OCD beliefs. Instead of reassuring someone that they have nothing to worry about, encourage them to gather their own evidence that this is the case. Ask them whether there are any thought challenges or behavioural experiments that they are able to do to help them overcome this worry. Perhaps find out if there is a way you can help or support them with this process instead of offering reassurance. For example, try saying to them: 'I'm not going to reassure you about that as it won't help. However, I think getting some evidence to prove that this isn't something you need to worry about would be beneficial – is this something I can help with?'

NB: Be careful not to be drawn into doing the behavioural experiment for someone as this could be a form of reassurance seeking/giving. However, perhaps you could work with someone, help them, take something off them so they have the time to test it out for themselves.

By refusing to reassure them and encouraging the person with OCD to challenge their beliefs, you should see a reduction in OCD thinking, which in turn will result in a lot less anxiety. This is good news for both of you and makes the tricky part of stopping reassurance well worth it.

→ Remember to look after YOU

Sometimes we can get so caught up in worrying about the person with OCD and their anxieties that we forget to consider ourselves and how we are feeling. It is really important to remember to look after yourself as well as other people. Unless we feel strong and healthy, we are unable to support other people. Sometimes we feel as though we have a lot of responsibility and we just have to 'keep going'. However, we are not robots. It is unrealistic to think that you can live with something as stressful as OCD in your household and that it won't affect you in some way and so we need to look after ourselves, as well as the person with the diagnosis.

TAKE TIME FOR YOU

It is really important to keep a focus on your own wellbeing and things that make you feel happy, fulfilled and confident. Make sure that you are putting some time aside for yourself, even if that means leaving the person with OCD to fend for themselves for an hour while you have break.

The OCD is not going to go away overnight. This is a marathon not a sprint. Imagine if you were training for an actual marathon. You wouldn't jump on a treadmill and just keep running without stopping – you'd very quickly become exhausted and burn out. Instead you would train and take regular rest, eat healthily, take care of yourself and ensure that you were in top condition. Dealing with OCD is the same. You need to look after yourself and ensure you are happy and healthy, as well as the person with the OCD.

SAY NO TO UNREASONABLE DEMANDS

Sometimes with OCD we forget that it is okay to say no. We may be so used to doing things for the person with OCD we may have lost sight of what is reasonable. Try keeping a log of what you are being asked to do as this will help you figure out what is reasonable and what you need to say 'no' to.

REMEMBER YOU CAN'T DO IT FOR THEM

Sometimes we can feel that if we just give someone the extra support, or that extra boost of confidence then maybe they will seek help or get better. However, it is important to remember that we cannot force someone to change. While it is great to offer someone support and encouragement, we cannot make someone make positive changes or seek help for their OCD. The only thing we can control is how we respond and how we look after ourselves and so it is important to do so.

By looking after ourselves we will be stronger and more able to help someone else. If we feel weak and worn out by the situation then we won't be able to encourage and support them to make positive changes. Therefore remember to take care of yourself and implement some of the strategies in this chapter to help you give up some of the exhausting behaviours, and focus on positive challenging and changing behaviours.

Key points to remember

- ▶ By separating the two out and recognizing that it is absolutely normal and reasonable to be fed up and angry with that person's OCD, this will help you to get rid of some of the guilt and blame you put on yourself. It is ok to be angry with OCD.

- ▶ Reassurance does not help OCD in the long term. Although it may provide some short-term relief, ultimately it only feeds the OCD beliefs and is not helpful for someone trying to overcome their OCD.

- ▶ Encourage someone to challenge and gain evidence against their OCD beliefs. This is more effective than reassurance seeking and results in reduced future anxiety.

Where to next?

This chapter has looked at the impact of OCD on others and how FFC can help and support those with OCD on their journey to better health. The next chapter focuses on life after OCD and considers strategies for preventing relapse. Again, this next chapter may be useful for those around the person with OCD, as well as the individual with the diagnosis themselves.

12 Enjoying life without OCD: relapse prevention

. . . .

About this chapter

▶ This chapter focuses on life after OCD, and what might get in the way of living 'OCD-free'. This chapter also considers some relapse prevention strategies to help you to manage any future anxieties that may trigger OCD symptoms, including completing a relapse-prevention worksheet.

. . . .

→ I have had OCD for so long that I've forgotten who I am without it – help!

Think back to Chapter 4 when we looked at who you were before OCD. We know that living with OCD is an all-encompassing experience, and that the OCD may have affected so many areas of your life that it is now hard to picture what day-to-day living looks like without it. OCD takes over a big part of your identity and it can feel as though we've lost ourselves, with our own identity buried beneath the OCD. Once you have overcome your OCD and taken control back, it is important to establish who you are without it. OCD gets in the way of a lot of things such as spontaneity and fun and it can prevent us from taking advantage of opportunities. If this has been the case for you then now is the time to re-establish who you are and uncover your own identity again – without OCD.

⏰ Exercise 36

Write down the top ten things that OCD has prevented you from doing that you've always wanted to do – then turn them into your new 'to do' list (it may help to remember your SMART goal principles here).

My top ten OCD-free to do list:

1 _____

_____

_____

2 _____

_____

_____

3 _____

_____

_____

4 _____

_____

_____

5 _____

_____

_____

6 _____

_____

_____

7 _____

_____

_____

8 _____

_____

_____

9 _____

_____

_____

10 _____

_____

_____

Keep future focused – what else is possible now that your OCD is under control? What else can you do in the future that you never thought possible? What would you like to achieve in a year or so? Keep some longer goals in mind as well as immediate short-term goals.

Remember to monitor and review your goals continuously. This will help keep you on track and motivated for moving forwards.

→ I'm almost better now … can I stop challenging myself now?

One of the difficulties in overcoming OCD is that as you start to feel better, life improves dramatically, and so it is tempting not to complete treatment. As you find yourself able to do things that you haven't been able to do for years, OCD is dramatically reduced and you find that your life is your own once more. This feeling naturally brings with it a sense of elation and joy which is wonderful, but often getting over anxiety means we are reluctant to ever experience it again.

This reluctance then means that we tolerate a low-level anxiety because it is so much better than the acute anxiety we had been living with previously. This reluctance also means that we stop challenging our OCD thinking and actions because they become low level and infrequent and so we tolerate them, rather than deliberately evoke feelings of stronger anxiety.

You may be thinking 'what's the problem? A tiny bit of anxiety is miles better than what I've put up with over the past few years'. In order to understand why this is a problem I want you to imagine that your mind is a garden. Before you started to treat your OCD this garden was overrun with weeds, each weed representing an OCD thought/ belief. When you start to overcome OCD it is as though you are pulling these weeds out by the root, killing off the OCD-driven beliefs one by one, leaving your garden looking weed-free, clear and beautiful once more. As you know from challenging the OCD, some of those weeds were stubborn with tough roots, and as any lazy gardener (like me!) will know, sometimes it's tempting to just mow over the weeds without killing the root, so that the garden looks better.

So what happens to the garden if we don't pull weeds out by the root? It looks better for a while but slowly and surely some of the weeds creep back up. We can ignore them at first and admire the rest of the garden but after a while the weeds get higher and higher and they scramble over the rest of the garden and all your hard work was in vain and you feel back to square one.

The same is true of your OCD. If we don't challenge and change all our OCD-driven thoughts and behaviours then it is as though we are leaving our mind-garden vulnerable to the thoughts coming back.

I always say to people – 'don't get 50% better'. I appreciate that is easier said than done but trust me – you want to completely weed the garden and get rid of OCD once and for all. This also means being aware in the future of any potential weeds blowing into your garden and being mindful of what state your garden is in. If you begin to feel stressed or anxious in response to life events/situations at work and so on, then just cast your eye over your garden – is it weed free?

Thinking honestly about where you feel you are now – does it feel as though you are OCD free? If not, what is left to challenge? Make a note of your 'weeds' and work on a plan to continue to challenge these. Although it can be frustrating to even give OCD the time of day when we feel better, trust me – this is the path to success!

→ The new you in old relationships

Sometimes people are so used to seeing our OCD that they forget to see past it and notice us as we actually are. This means that introducing the new 'OCD-free' you to people who have only known your OCD can feel quite daunting and difficult. We often look very different without OCD and so it can be hard for people to adjust to the changes that we make once we get better. Consider the tips below to help you bring a new, OCD-free you into your existing relationships.

Exercise 37

The first step to introducing people to the new you is to be clear about what has changed and what you now expect from them. This is extremely important because while we feel very different on the inside, very little will have changed on the outside, and as we know people are not mind readers. Therefore they may be completely unaware of how differently you are feeling.

Think about someone who you are in a relationship with, whether that be a friendship, a working relationship or a romantic relationship. Now consider some of the things that may have changed for you in this relationship as a result of you tackling your anxiety.

Complete the sheet below to help you summarize this information:

Relationship: *Partner*	
When I was anxious	Now I am not anxious
e.g. used to check things for me	I know it is unhelpful and so want to check things myself.

SHARE THE INFORMATION

Although it can feel exposing it is important to share the information you have identified above with others. Ask someone to spend some time with you going through the list and highlighting the changes that you have made, and how you would like things to be different. Also encourage them to make their own list of things that they used to do for you/their OCD so that they can ask you what is and isn't expected of them anymore.

THEY CAN'T SEEM TO ACCEPT THE NEW ME – WHAT DO I DO?

Sometimes we can feel as though we are a completely different person without OCD and the changes that we want to make can feel extreme to others.

First, try to have a conversation together asking the person to name some of their concerns/reluctances. Some of the most common difficulties that people face are listed below. If you get stuck in your conversation, use these as prompts to guide you. Ask the person you are in a relationship with to look at the list and highlight any that are familiar to them.

Common reasons for struggling to adapt:

1   *We've been here before*. OCD fluctuates and often this means that people have seen you make progress before but then struggled with your OCD. This fluctuating nature of the OCD means it can be difficult for people to feel these changes are different/more permanent.

2   *I don't know how much to help*. It may be that your partner/friend/ colleague has got used to doing everything for you and the idea of handing back that responsibility may feel too much for them. They may be worried about how much to help and worry about overwhelming you/making you feel worse.

3   *What do I do if you get anxious again?* For many people they don't know what to do for the best when someone they care about is feeling anxious and they worry about making the situation worse. They may also be concerned about triggering OCD thoughts or feel as though they are treading on eggshells around you, which is uncomfortable for you both.

4   *I can't trust you anymore*. Although hard to hear sometimes, people can feel as though they have had to take on extra responsibility or handle situations that you have been unable to manage with your OCD. This means they can feel as though they are the only person who can handle them. Also when we have been highly anxious we may have broken promises or been unable to complete tasks due to our OCD becoming too much to cope with. This means it can be difficult to trust that we can do something when we say we feel better now.

→ How to overcome these barriers

⊕ *Exercise 38*

Now that you have identified the barriers that get in the way, the key is to keep discussing these. Tell someone what you would like to achieve, where you think you might need help and support and what you anticipate their role being in it. Use the worksheet below to help you (an example has been given as a guide):

I would like to: (e.g. get the children ready for bed)

_____

_____

_____

_____

_____

_____

_____

_____

_____

I might need help with: (e.g. usual evening chores to allow me time to do this)

_____

_____

_____

_____

_____

_____

_____

_____

_____

_____

I would like you to: (e.g. remind me that I can do it and to challenge my OCD thoughts. DO NOT offer to help me or do it for me, this is something I need to do for myself, even if it takes me longer than it would take you.)

_____

_____

_____

_____

_____

_____

_____

_____

_____

By being open and honest about what you hope to achieve and what you would and wouldn't like help with, you are helping someone else understand how you are feeling and what they can do to help. This should make things a lot clearer and easier for someone else to adapt to.

→ Beware old habits

When you first start overcoming your anxiety you may catch yourself making thinking errors or starting to become anxious before you apply the techniques that you have learned throughout this book. This is because your mind will have formed a habit of OCD thinking and so it will automatically start to think OCD thoughts about a situation.

If this happens to you then be kind to yourself. There is no point adding criticism and guilt to your feelings of anxiety. Instead just acknowledge that it will take a bit more time to break the habit and then apply one or more of the techniques learned to help reduce your OCD symptoms.

To begin with you will need to make a conscious effort to retrain your thinking to new paths that are logical and evidence based not anxiety based. However, after a very short while your brain will form new thinking habits and this will become automatic.

→ What if my OCD comes back?

One of the things that can hold us back is the fear of OCD coming back again. Sometimes we are worried about trying anything new or challenging ourselves in case it triggers the OCD to come back and we feel overwhelmed again. If this is you, then remember some of the key points listed below:

THIS IS AN ANXIOUS BELIEF

The worry about OCD coming back if you push yourself too far is an anxiety-driven belief – so challenge it! Push yourself further and see what happens.

YOU NEVER GO BACK TO SQUARE ONE

The idea of going back to square one can feel very intimidating but it's important to remember that you never go back to square one. Now you know what a bully OCD is, how it affects you and the strategies to overcome it, you are in a much better position than you were before. You are better equipped, stronger and more confident than you were before you started tackling anxiety. You may experience a relapse but you will never go back to square one.

CONSIDER STEPS FOR RELAPSE PREVENTION

The next part of this chapter focuses on a relapse prevention worksheet, which will help you plan for any setbacks and allow you to develop a clear blueprint or plan for what to do in case this happens.

→ # Relapse prevention

I'M STARTING TO FEEL THE OCD AGAIN – WHAT DO I DO?

First of all, if you are feeling anxious then be kind to yourself. We all experience intrusive thoughts and anxiety and you are allowed to feel anxious. The important thing is that you have recognized that this is OCD, which means you are now in a strong position to do something about it. Therefore, rather than tell yourself off for being anxious, acknowledge your OCD thinking and reward yourself for taking the first steps to overcome it.

I THOUGHT I WAS OVER OCD – WHY AM I FEELING ANXIOUS NOW?

It is not possible to live life *completely* free of anxiety. This is because life events will occur that cause us to have understandable feelings of anxiety and worry. As a result you may feel OCD thinking and behaviours starting to creep in.

Exercise 39

It is important to realize that you are not going back to square one here. You have skills and experience now that will protect you from relapses. First, let's formally identify what has happened recently that has led to your anxiety. Use the table below to help you.

What am I feeling anxious about?	What has happened recently to make me feel this way?	What impact is this having on me?	What would I like to be able to do in this situation instead of feeling anxious?
e.g. germs and contamination	I watched a TV show about cleaning and now I feel as though everything around me and my children is dirty	I keep checking they aren't touching anything that looks dirty and I am washing their hands and toys a lot more often	I'd like to challenge the idea that the world around me is dirty so that I can relax and enjoy life again without the OCD creeping back up

Listen to what OCD is telling you to do... then do the opposite! It is essential to continue to challenge the OCD thoughts. If OCD tells you not to walk into a room, then charge into that room without a backward glance – yes you can!

⏱ *Exercise 40*

Use the relapse prevention worksheet below as a guide to remind you how to deal with your OCD. Keep this somewhere safe so that you have access to it when you feel OCD creeping back in.

Relapse Prevention Worksheet

Before I started this process I felt ...

(e.g. include here how you felt when you were living with OCD)

_____

_____

_____

_____

_____

_____

_____

_____

_____

Coming towards the end of this book I feel ...

(e.g. make a note here of how you feel given the changes you have made and the strategies you have put in place)

_____

_____

_____

_____

_____

_____

_____

_____

_____

I want to continue working towards …

(e.g. write here what you wish to continue to aim for in the future. Note situations or circumstances in which you would like to be different, and note any particular goals or forthcoming events that you can work towards)

_____

_____

_____

_____

_____

_____

_____

_____

_____

_____

I know that potential triggers for me feeling anxious are …

(e.g. note down the potential situations or circumstances that may trigger anxiety and OCD-related thoughts and/or behaviours in the future)

_____

_____

_____

_____

_____

_____

_____

_____

_____

The strategies I have learned for dealing with these triggers are ...

(e.g. write down here all the strategies that you have learned. This should act as a summary list of the strategies you have learned and how you can use them to tackle this problem)

_____

_____

_____

_____

_____

_____

_____

_____

_____

Whenever I feel OCD creeping back in I will do the following ...

(e.g. use this space to write out a clear plan of what you will do next time you feel this way.

For example your plan may be: 1. look for the evidence of these thoughts; 2. set a SMART goal to help me deal with this situation; 3. reward myself and prioritize pleasurable activity.

The aim of this section is that when we feel strong emotions it can be difficult to think logically and rationally and so if you have a pre-written plan you can simply refer to this rather than have to try to remember everything when feeling anxious)

_____

_____

_____

_____

_____

_____

_____

_____

My motivation for continuing to work on this is ...

(e.g. think about your end goal(s) and what you want to achieve)

_____

_____

_____

_____

_____

_____

_____

_____

_____

I know it is important that I …

(e.g. write down here key lessons that you have learned. These are not so much specific strategies as more general issues that are important, e.g. 'take time out for myself', 'ask for help', 'remember to reward myself for achievements')

_____

_____

_____

_____

_____

_____

_____

_____

_____

_____

In a year I want to be …

(e.g. do a bit of time travelling and imagine yourself a year from now free from OCD. The aim of this is to give you a longer-term focus and help you picture the future and what you are aiming for)

_____

_____

_____

_____

_____

_____

_____

_____

_____

In five years I want to be …

(e.g. similar to above, imagine yourself five years from now and think about what you would like to be doing in five years)

_____

_____

_____

_____

_____

_____

_____

_____

_____

Key points to remember

▶ It is normal to experience some anxiety or worry in response to life events and this does not mean that you are back to square one. Remember you are now more skilled in challenging and overcoming your OCD.

▶ Keep your relapse prevention worksheet somewhere handy so that you can turn to it when you feel OCD thoughts or behaviours creeping in.

▶ You can overcome this – it is only your OCD that tells you that you can't. You are stronger than your anxiety.

Where to next?

This chapter concludes the workbook sections and you have completed your journey out of OCD. Now is your time to enjoy some time for you without OCD. Reward yourself for completing the workbook, wave goodbye to your OCD and go and enjoy your life on your own terms, leaving OCD behind.

13

Your top OCD questions answered

▶ Prior to writing this book I appealed to those affected by OCD to ask me what they wanted me to include in this book, and what they would find most helpful. The responses to these questions have been addressed throughout the chapters of this workbook and I hope they have provided some practical answers to reader queries. While one or two have been highlighted, the majority have been answered throughout the workbook.

This section is looking at specific issues that I wanted to discuss, which haven't fitted into other chapters.

→ Why is my anticipatory anxiety so much worse than the actual feared event?

The person who emailed me this described a situation where he could not tolerate the anticipated anxiety around his thought process of whether or not he would touch an electric fence. He described how he then went over and deliberately grabbed the electric fence with both hands in order to 'get it over with' and stop the anxiety from building in his mind. He felt that by grasping the fence with both hands he had prevented himself from questioning whether or not he would accidentally brush against it and the anxiety that this would bring with it.

This is an interesting issue that I'm sure many people can relate to. A sense of rather than dreading something possibly happening, getting it over with and then you can stop worrying about it as it's too late and has happened. This relates to the idea of intolerance of uncertainty. The uncertainty over whether or not he might accidentally brush against the fence became too much and was intolerable and so he found it better to grasp the fence with both hands, than continue to feel the doubt and uncertainty.

This is an understandable reaction as individuals who experience high anxiety will be driven to do lots of things to avoid it, even extreme actions that they don't wish to do, such as touching the electric fence, which may cause considerable discomfort.

When used the right way, this direct approach to not tolerating uncertainty can be good to use as a way of challenging the OCD thoughts (see Chapter 8) on thought challenging. However, it is not always possible or desirable to achieve certainty in this way. It is much better to learn to tolerate the uncertainty than to need to seek certainty every time. See previous chapters on learning to tolerate uncertainty.

→ Don't get frustrated or give up – it may work next time!

It is possible that you have already attempted therapy and found it unhelpful and are feeling, understandably, demotivated and a bit hopeless about the future. This is an understandable reaction, but I wanted to spend a bit of time briefly thinking about why therapy might have been unsuccessful as there are many factors that affect successful therapy.

DID YOU LIKE YOUR THERAPIST?

This might sound a bit trite but actually it is really important that you trust your therapist 100 per cent and are able to tell them everything. Therefore if you started working with someone but you didn't have faith in what they were doing, or you felt unable to disclose to them, then therapy won't have worked.

WAS IT THE RIGHT TIME?

Sometimes when we start therapy it is because others have encouraged us to attend or have threatened consequences if we don't.

WAS IT THE RIGHT THERAPY?

Lots of people claim to have had 'CBT' but when you look at the basics of what they covered in their session it wasn't CBT at all. It is important to ask about your therapist's qualifications and experience in working with OCD before working with them.

Go back and review the chapter on preparing for therapy and check that this is the best time for you to be undergoing therapy. Was this the case last time? In order to make changes in therapy it needs to be the right time and the right person so don't despair if you've tried therapy before and it hasn't been successful – it may well be next time. In addition to this I also wanted to include the email below, which I received regarding therapy and therapy outcomes.

I received an email from a lady who had had successful therapy and, with her permission, I am including it below. Although this is just one person's experience, I believe that she has captured a great deal in her email. She also discusses why some things hadn't worked for her, which I think is very useful.

Case study A

I had OCD for many years before receiving exceptionally good quality CBT, which made a massive difference to my life. Prior to that I had tried using self-help books and spent some years on various NHS waiting lists from which the only outcome was four sessions of very poor quality CBT on one occasion and an offer of sessions with a counsellor (who openly said that she knew very little about OCD) on another occasion.

One key observation on the good quality CBT was that, rather than mere exposure and response therapy to 'wear down' one's anxiety response, they took me through a process of doing tasks that were designed to show me that I'd actually created this understanding of the world for myself, and that it wasn't imposed by some external source that I had to comply with to keep everything safe. Once I realized that it was actually my head that had come up with this perception of how the world worked, I could see, then, that it would in fact be possible to challenge that thinking and try out different approaches to my response to 'OCD situations'. I think that even though one knows that OCD is a mis-held belief and doesn't really make any sense, in the absence of any other understanding it is still a 'belief'. I think that reaching the point where I believed that that thinking could be changed was key to the CBT being successful for me.

In contrast to the self-help books that I had tried, the approaches put forward just seemed to be about trying 'Not' to do OCD things and recording how you felt, to learn that through time and exposure and response activities one would realize that the level of anxiety felt in an OCD response was reducing.

Basically, I don't think I could really see what the books were asking me to do – if I could have tried 'not to do OCD things', I would have (and was trying to do so even before working through a book), but the fact was that I believed that I needed to do them even though I knew other people didn't need to and it didn't properly make sense, the risk was just too great.

Whether it was because OCD was pretty ingrained in me at the time of reading the books (I'd had OCD since primary school but not found out that it was a known 'thing' until I was about 20) or otherwise, the fact that I'd not gone through a process of understanding that I could challenge OCD thinking as I'd given myself the rules and they weren't some kind of special responsibility placed on me in life from something external, meant that I couldn't engage in the processes the books were trying to guide me through.

The good therapy that I received first dealt with my understanding of the fact that, for whatever reason, I'd adopted an unhelpful way of thinking with regard to how the world worked, before then going on to the business of trying OCD triggering things and looking at how they affected me and alternative ways of understanding that response.

Anyway, the first time I walked down a street in town that I'd avoided for three or four years, I was on edge but I wanted to do it. When I reached the street, walked along it and realized that I was even free to walk into a shop on the street if I wanted to … I realized that I had a big grin on my face, which was not at all what I'd expected. What's more, the feeling of taking just one step towards the freedom that I'd got from that experience made me want more and want to try challenging other stuff.

Eventually, too, I think that this approach teaches one's brain to think differently, rather than just learning to bear a feeling of anxiety (which might creep back over time). Like learning to drive a car, once your brain knows how to do it (think differently) you can't then not know.

Hopefully, the above email offers good insight into some of the factors that work for others, and these can be applied to your own therapy journey.

→ If I seek treatment then am I a bad person for wanting these 'pure', 'good' thoughts to stop?

If I stop wanting to have good thoughts/questioning my sin then am I a bad person?

This was an issue that quite a few people emailed me about. The main issue seemed to be a concern around wanting the OCD thoughts to stop, but worrying that if they were thoughts around scrupulosity e.g. not sinning, not being a bad person, etc. then did wanting the thoughts to stop make them a bad person?

Exercise 41

We can recognize a few thinking errors in this statement but this can also be linked to some unhelpful beliefs we hold about the purpose of worrying. Review the table below and see if any apply to you:

Beliefs about the function of worry and what it means to worry – if I stop worrying then have I stopped caring?

Unhelpful belief about worry	What it means	Is this your belief? (✓)
Worry helps me to prepare	Often when people talk about their worry they talk about it serving a protective purpose. It is as though the act of worrying somehow prepares you for the worst-case scenario and this means that you are able to prepare and plan ahead for this eventuality.	
Worry makes me a better parent/partner/employee	When people discuss worrying making them a better person, often they are referring to the fact that worrying shows that they care. E.g. people believe that if they worry about their children then they are just being a responsible parent and that this shows how much they love their children.	

If I worry then I can prevent bad things happening as God/fate/destiny will not interfere	This belief often links to a belief around external control, with people believing that if they worry then God/fate/destiny will see that they care and have thought about something and therefore nothing bad will happen.	
Worry keeps me going	People often believe that a little bit of worry and stress keeps them going and motivated meaning they achieve more; e.g. an individual may believe that worrying about losing their job ensures that they work harder and achieve more at work.	
Worry keeps me one step ahead	This belief highlights how people feel worrying gives them the edge. That they are already one step ahead of life-events and have prepared for several different scenarios and are prepared for anything. This sense of being prepared for day-to-day life can also help us to feel a lot more in control day-to-day.	

You may have recognized several beliefs about worry that you hold and you may be concerned about letting the worry go. However, we know from working through this workbook that this is simply anxious thinking and so we need to challenge these beliefs about worry and gain a more balanced perspective.

Use the table below to help you challenge some of these unhelpful beliefs about worry:

Belief about worry	Questions to help you challenge this belief
Worry helps me to prepare	When you worry are you able to make clear and concise plans? Or does your mind simply race around worst-case scenarios? Do you need to spend your time preparing for scenarios that might never happen? Would your energy not be better spent preparing for scenarios that you know will happen, and things that you want to achieve, rather than being spent preparing for eventualities that may never occur? Does worry really help you feel any more prepared?
Worry makes me a better parent/partner/employee	Does the actual act of worrying really make you a better person and show you care? Is it possible that while you are spending so much time worrying, you are not paying attention to what is actually happening, and therefore might miss something important at work/home/school? While meaning to be more careful, does worrying in fact make you distracted and forgetful? Does worrying actually make you feel so overwhelmed that you cannot cope?

If I worry then I can prevent bad things happening as God/fate/destiny will not interfere	Do you really hold any power over any of these things? Do you really believe that God/fate/destiny is malevolent and will punish you unless you worry about these things considerably? Do you have any evidence that this is the case?
Worry keeps me going	Can you be motivated without worrying? Wouldn't more confidence in yourself be a better motivator than fear of failure? Have you any evidence that says you cannot achieve success without worrying? As mentioned above, is it possible that actually worrying so much means you miss out on bigger opportunities as you are too bogged down in worrying? Does worry push you or hinder you?
Worry keeps me one step ahead	Do you need to worry to be prepared for the day ahead? Do other people worry excessively in order to prepare for the day ahead? If not, what do they do instead? Do you need to worry to prepare? Wouldn't you feel more energized, confident and relaxed for the day ahead if you could stop worrying?

→ Can OCD be a good thing?

One very interesting email that I received was from a man who asked me to discuss the more positive elements of OCD. You can read his (edited) email below:

Case study B

I am a long-term OCD 'sufferer' but regard it in a positive light. For example, a large component of it for me is order and tidiness. I have always felt that this raises the standard in the home while my family members benefit from my activities of shoe arranging and the like!

My aversion to certain contaminants makes me the chief bottle washer and tidy upperer.

I also have a hoarding component to my OCD and this makes me quite frugal and careful of waste – so recycling, etc. did not come as a shock to our household.

While I agree that the media trivializes OCD, I still think there is room for some positivity in terms of coping strategies (as outlined above).

I hope this goes some way to giving you an alternative view for your book as well as some help for minor sufferers who perhaps flog themselves in a typically British fashion instead of seeing what maybe IS good about (mild) OCD.

I wanted to include this perspective in my book because I think it is important to differentiate between those who believe they experience OCD 'symptoms' and OCD itself. It is not uncommon to express a desire or a need for orderliness and cleanliness. This in itself is not OCD. It is very possible to want to live a more organized, cleaner and regimented lifestyle than most, and this still would not necessitate a diagnosis of OCD.

Part of the diagnostic criteria, that is, part of what tells us whether someone has OCD or not, is the level of distress they experience. Those diagnosed with OCD will experience significant distress by what they are doing and will find their OCD behaviours significantly impact on their day, and prevent them from getting on with day-to-day life. Also, those with OCD find their behaviours and compulsions can involve them for up to an hour or more per day.

Those who do not experience distress from their symptoms may experience a preference for order and cleanliness and they may hold some fear or disgust around contamination and germs. However, I would question the idea of 'enjoying' OCD. If the distress is not present then this isn't OCD. Also, although people may feel those around them benefit from their high standards and behaviours, it is important to recognize that those around us are entitled to their own standards and beliefs as well. If these don't match our high standards, then this doesn't make them wrong, it makes them different. This is important to remember if we share our home with others, as they may not actually be benefiting from our high standards as much as we like.

The idea of a desire for cleanliness, orderliness and routine leads nicely into an explanation of **Obsessive Compulsive Personality Disorder (OCPD)** and how it differs from OCD.

→ A brief explanation of the difference between OCD and OCPD

(The information below is taken from the International OCD Foundation factsheet regarding OCPD):

WHAT IS OBSESSIVE COMPULSIVE PERSONALITY DISORDER (OCPD)?

OCPD is a type of 'personality disorder' with the following characteristics:

- A rigid adherence to rules and regulations
- An overwhelming need for order
- An unwillingness to yield or give responsibilities to others
- A sense of righteousness about the way things 'should be done'.

WHAT ARE THE SYMPTOMS OF OCPD?

▶ Excessive devotion to work that impairs social and family activities

▶ Excessive fixation with lists, rules and minor details

▶ Perfectionism that interferes with finishing tasks

▶ Rigid following of moral and ethical codes

▶ Unwillingness to assign tasks unless others perform exactly as asked

▶ Lack of generosity; extreme frugality without reason

▶ Hoarding behaviours.

The diagnosis of OCPD is made when these traits result in a significant impairment in social, work and/or family functioning. A person does not need to have all of these symptoms to have the personality disorder.

WHAT IS THE DIFFERENCE BETWEEN OCPD AND OCD?

▶ People with OCD have insight, meaning they are aware that their unwanted thoughts are unreasonable. People with OCPD think their way is the 'right and best way' and usually feel comfortable with such self-imposed systems of rules.

▶ The thoughts, behaviours and feared consequences common to OCD are typically not relevant to real-life concerns; people with OCPD are fixated with following procedures to manage daily tasks.

▶ Often, OCD interferes in several areas in the person's life including work, social and/or family life. OCPD usually interferes with interpersonal relationships, but makes work functioning more efficient. It is not the job itself that is hurt by OCPD traits, but the relationships with co-workers, or even employers can be strained.

▶ Typically, people with OCPD don't believe they require treatment. They believe that if everyone else conformed to their strict rules, things would be fine! The threat of losing a job or a relationship due to interpersonal conflict may be the motivator for therapy. This is in contrast to people with OCD who feel tortured by their unwanted thoughts and rituals, and are more aware of the unreasonable demands that the symptoms place on others, often feeling guilty because of this.

▶ Family members of people with OCPD often feel extremely criticized and controlled by people with OCPD. Similar to living with someone with OCD, being ruled under OCPD demands can be very frustrating and upsetting, often leading to conflict.

→ Do sportsmen and sportswomen have OCD?

When the Olympics were in London, the media was alive with how athletes prepare, with specialist diets and often talked about pre-race rituals or 'good luck' charms. The idea of rituals that need to be completed to prevent a disastrous outcome (e.g. not winning) made some people question whether sports players are more prone to having/developing OCD than others. This is an interesting issue and one that has prompted continual on going research.

When researching an article for OCD-UK, I spoke to several professional rugby players who were familiar with the idea of pre-game rituals, and the impact they could have. Although this is by no means extensive or completed research, some of the ideas they discussed with me have been included below, mainly as food for thought rather than providing any conclusive evidence.

▶ Rituals were common. Most of the players I spoke to had some pre-match ritual that they went through before training/playing an important game.

▶ Some of these rituals involved other people. One player said that he had to say hello and shake the hand of every member of the team before going on to the pitch. He couldn't really say what he thought would happen if he didn't do this before a game. It was more that he wouldn't feel 'right' and that it would bother him.

▶ They developed at a time of high responsibility. Most of the players I spoke to were recruited at the age of 15 or 16 years old and were immediately thrown into a world of elite athletics, high-pressure training and huge responsibilities, i.e. they had to win! All of the players talked about how they had found the experience incredible, but also hugely pressurizing. They felt that nothing really prepared them for it, and that they had to shoulder a lot of responsibility at a young age. The players I spoke to said that they developed these rituals as coping strategies, things that made them feel more in control of the game.

▶ If they didn't complete the ritual and didn't win then they would attribute that to forgetting their ritual. However, if they won they did not attribute success to the completion of the ritual.

▶ Rituals were an accepted part of pre-game. Players reported that some people went off on their own for a few minutes to mentally prepare whereas others had very vocal rituals that included everyone. Although there was some gentle banter, no one seemed to think pre-game rituals were odd, or questionable, even those that seemed more extreme. One player reported: 'I have to touch everything in the room. It drives me mad but if I don't do it I feel all wrong. Sometimes even if we're running late or our trainer is talking to me I still have to run around touching everything.'

▶ Some players felt others did take things a bit far and self-reported that they felt other players exhibited OCD. There was a sense of 'I'm alright and my rituals are "normal" but you should see some of the guys!'. There was a reluctance to question own rituals – they were just a part of the game.

▶ As there were no consequences and they were well-accommodated, no single player I spoke to saw the point in stopping the rituals. 'I know it's just superstition but I do think there's something in it. Even if it's nonsense I don't want to stop ... just in case.' This is very different to those I speak to who have OCD who believe more strongly that their rituals are not helpful and desperately want to stop, although the feeling of not being able to 'just in case' is shared across athletes and those with OCD.

As you can see, there are some shared characteristics between the behaviour of those with OCD and those playing professional sport. However, my brief interviews are not enough to conclude whether or not sports professionals are more or less likely to develop OCD. Research into this very interesting topic is ongoing and will no doubt be highlighted in the media in the near future.

Bibliography

American Psychiatric Association. (2013), *Diagnostic and statistical manual of mental disorders* (5th ed.). Arlington, VA: American Psychiatric Publishing.

Beck, A., (1976), *Cognitive Therapy and the Emotional Disorders*, Oxford, UK: International Universities Press.

Doran, G.T., (1981), 'There's a S.M.A.R.T. way to write management's goals and objectives', *Management Review*, 70, 11: 35–36.

Fitzgerald, S., (2013), *The Beating Anxiety Workbook*, Hodder & Stoughton.

Foa, E.B., Huppert, J.D., Leiberg, S., Langner, R., Kichic, R., Hajcak, G., & Salkovskis, P.M., (2002), The Obsessive-Compulsive Inventory: Development and validation of a short version, *Psychological Assessment*, 14: 485–496

Padesky, C.A. & Mooney, K.A., (1990), Clinical Tips: Presenting the Cognitive Model to Clients, *International Cognitive Therapy Newsletter*, 6: 13–14.

Rachman, S.J., (1997), A cognitive theory of obsessions, *Behaviour Research and Therapy*, 35: 793-802

Rachman, S.J., & Shafran, R., (1999), Cognitive distortions: Thought-action fusion, *Clinical Psychology and Psychotherapy*, 6: 80-85

Salkovskis, P.M., (1985) Obsessional-compulsive problems: A cognitive-behavioural analysis, *Behaviour Research and Therapy*, 23: 571–583.

Salkovskis, P.M., (1996), Cognitive-behavioural approaches to the understanding of obsessional problems. In Rapee, R.M., *Current controversies in the anxiety disorders*, (pp 103–133), New York: Guildford Press.

Salkovskis, P.M., (1985), Understanding and treating obsessive-compulsive disorder, *Behaviour Research and Therapy*, 37: 29–52.

Salkovskis, P.M., Forrester, E. & Richards, C., (1998), Cognitive-behavioural approach to understanding obsessional thinking, *British Journal of Psychiatry*, 173, 35: 53–63.

Wolpe, J., (1958), *Psychotherapy by reciprocal inhibition*, Stanford, CA: Stanford University Press.

Useful contacts

OCD-UK
PO Box 8955
Nottingham
NG10 9AU
T: 0845 120 3778
Website: www.ocduk.org
Email: support@ocduk.org

Maternal OCD
Website: http://www.maternalocd.org/
Email: info@maternalocd.org

OCD Foundation
Website: http://www.ocfoundation.org/
Mailing Address:
International OCD Foundation, Inc.
P.O. Box 961029
Boston, MA 02196
USA
T: (617) 973-5801
F: (617) 973-5803
Email: info@iocdf.org

Mind
15–19 Broadway
Stratford
London
E15 4BQ
T: 020 8519 2122
F: 020 8522 1725
Website: www.mind.org.uk
Email: contact@mind.org.uk

NICE website: http://www.nice.org.uk

To access OCD Treatment Guidelines link to https://www.nice.org.uk/
guidance/CG31/chapter/introduction. Alternatively visit: www.nice.
org.uk and enter 'OCD' in the search box. This will bring up the NICE
guidelines for treatment of OCD.

Therapy Notebook

_____

_____

_____

_____

_____

_____

_____

_____

_____

_____

_____

_____

_____

_____

_____

_____

_____

Appendix

🕐 *Exercise 1*

Using the formulation diagram below, think of a situation (this doesn't necessarily need to be OCD related – this is just a practice exercise). Now draw out the situation considering how each of these areas was impacting on the others. An example has been given below to help you.

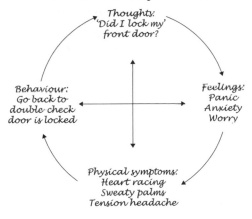

Situation: leaving the house

Thoughts:
'Did I lock my
front door?'

Feelings:
Panic
Anxiety
Worry

Physical symptoms:
Heart racing
Sweaty palms
Tension headache

Behaviour:
Go back to
double check
door is locked

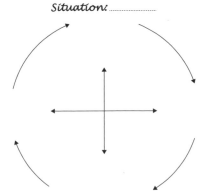

Situation: ....

Exercise 1

Using the formulation diagram below, think of a situation (this doesn't necessarily need to be OCD related – this is just a practice exercise). Now draw out the situation considering how each of these areas was impacting on the others. An example has been given below to help you.

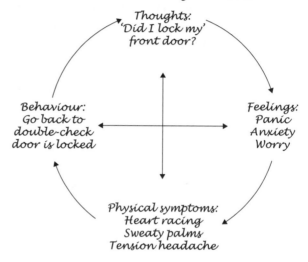

Situation: leaving the house

Thoughts:
'Did I lock my'
front door?

Feelings:
Panic
Anxiety
Worry

Physical symptoms:
Heart racing
Sweaty palms
Tension headache

Behaviour:
Go back to
double-check
door is locked

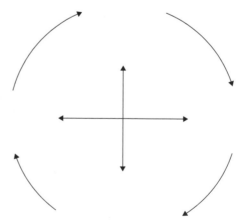

Situation: ....

🕐 *Exercise 2*

Work your way through the questionnaire and tick any symptoms that apply to you, then rate how much that symptom distresses you.

Symptom	Do you have this thought? (✓)	How much does this thought distress you?(0 = not at all, 1 = a little, 2 = moderately, 3 = a lot, 4 = extremely)
Unpleasant thoughts come into my mind against my will and I cannot get rid of them		
I think contact with bodily secretions (perspiration, saliva, blood, urine, etc.) may contaminate my clothing or somehow harm me		
I ask people to repeat things to me several times, even though I understood the first time		
I wash and clean obsessively		
I mentally go over past events, conversations and actions to make sure that I didn't do or say something wrong		
I have collected so many things that they get in the way		
I check things more often than necessary		
I avoid using public toilets because I am afraid of disease or contamination		
I repeatedly check doors, windows, drawers, etc.		
I repeatedly check gas and water taps and light switches after turning them off		

I collect things I don't need		
I have thoughts of having hurt someone without knowing it		
I have thoughts that I might want to harm myself or others		
I get upset if objects are not arranged properly		
I feel obliged to follow a certain order when undressing, dressing or washing myself		
I feel compelled to count while I am doing things		
I am afraid of impulsively doing embarrassing of harmful things		
I need to pray to cancel bad thoughts or feelings		
I keep on checking forms or other things I have written		
I get upset at the sight of scissors, knives and other sharp objects in case I lose control with them		
I am excessively concerned about cleanliness		
I find it difficult to touch an object when I know it has been touched by strangers or by certain people		
I need things to be arranged in a particular order		

⏰ Exercise 2

Work your way through the questionnaire and tick any symptoms that apply to you, then rate how much that symptom distresses you.

Symptom	Do you have this thought? (✓)	How much does this thought distress you?(0 = not at all, 1 = a little, 2 = moderately, 3 = a lot, 4 = extremely)
Unpleasant thoughts come into my mind against my will and I cannot get rid of them		
I think contact with bodily secretions (perspiration, saliva, blood, urine, etc.) may contaminate my clothing or somehow harm me		
I ask people to repeat things to me several times, even though I understood the first time		
I wash and clean obsessively		
I mentally go over past events, conversations and actions to make sure that I didn't do or say something wrong		
I have collected so many things that they get in the way		
I check things more often than necessary		
I avoid using public toilets because I am afraid of disease or contamination		
I repeatedly check doors, windows, drawers, etc.		
I repeatedly check gas and water taps and light switches after turning them off		

I collect things I don't need		
I have thoughts of having hurt someone without knowing it		
I have thoughts that I might want to harm myself or others		
I get upset if objects are not arranged properly		
I feel obliged to follow a certain order when undressing, dressing or washing myself		
I feel compelled to count while I am doing things		
I am afraid of impulsively doing embarrassing of harmful things		
I need to pray to cancel bad thoughts or feelings		
I keep on checking forms or other things I have written		
I get upset at the sight of scissors, knives and other sharp objects in case I lose control with them		
I am excessively concerned about cleanliness		
I find it difficult to touch an object when I know it has been touched by strangers or by certain people		
I need things to be arranged in a particular order		

Exercise 7

Use the space below to consider your own goals for overcoming OCD.

_____

_____

_____

_____

_____

_____

_____

_____

_____

_____

_____

_____

_____

_____

_____

_____

_____

Now reconsider the goals and use the table below to check if they follow SMART principles:

Goal	Specific ✓	Measurable ✓	Attainable ✓	Realistic ✓	Time limited ✓
e.g. write your goal here and then review it across the columns – does it meet the criteria?					

Once you have reviewed your goals and you are happy with them, make a copy of them and keep them somewhere visible. This helps keep your goals, and therefore your motivation, in mind and also encourages you to do something to work towards these goals every day.

Exercise 11

The diagram below is an example of what Adam's formulation looks like so far. Start to draw your own formulation out using the same headings – a blank formulation diagram has been included to help you.

Early experiences

(Making you vulnerable to OCD)
· Being told education is important
· Brother perceived as 'brighter'
· Can't tell anyone I'm struggling
· Secretive
· Negative family attitude
  towards laziness
· Long-term.

Critical incidents

(Starting this episode of OCD)
· Leaving home.

 Activates.

Assumptions and beliefs

· If I don't do extra work then I'll fail
· If I fail then I'll be kicked out
· If people find out I'm working extra
  hours then they'll think I'm stupid.
· Other people are brighter than me.

Intrusive thoughts/images/urges/doubts.

· 'I'm stupid'   · 'What if I've made a mistake?'
· 'I've done that wrong'   · 'This will be the one time
· 'I'd better check it'   it's wrong.'
· Urge to check.

Early experiences

Critical incidents

Activates.

Assumptions and beliefs

 Intrusive thoughts/images/urges/doubts.

Exercise 11

The diagram below is an example of what Adam's formulation looks like so far. Start to draw your own formulation out using the same headings – a blank formulation diagram has been included to help you.

Early experiences

(Making you vulnerable to OCD)
· Being told education is important
· Brother perceived as 'brighter'
· Can't tell anyone I'm struggling
· Secretive
· Negative family attitude
  towards laziness
· Long-term.

Critical incidents

(Starting this episode of OCD)
· Leaving home.

 Activates.

Assumptions and beliefs

· If I don't do extra work then I'll fail
· If I fail then I'll be kicked out
· If people find out I'm working extra
  hours then they'll think I'm stupid.
· Other people are brighter than me.

Intrusive thoughts/images/urges/doubts.

· 'I'm stupid'
· 'I've done that wrong'
· 'I'd better check it'
· Urge to check.

· 'What if I've made a mistake?'
· 'This will be the one time
  it's wrong.'

<u>*Early experiences*</u>

<u>*Critical incidents*</u>

Activates.

<u>*Assumptions and beliefs*</u>

<u>*Intrusive thoughts/images/urges/doubts.*</u>

Exercise 14

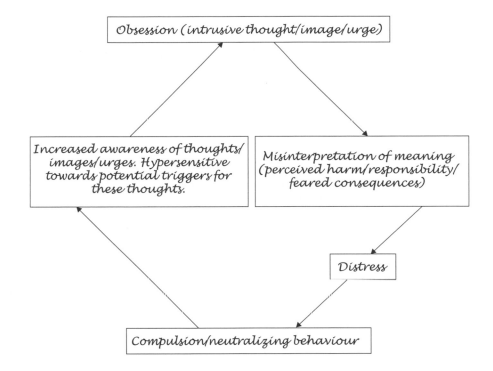

Looking at the model above, consider some of your own thoughts and behaviour and complete the CBT for OCD model for yourself. Work through the model using an example obsession that you struggle with and how this makes you feel.

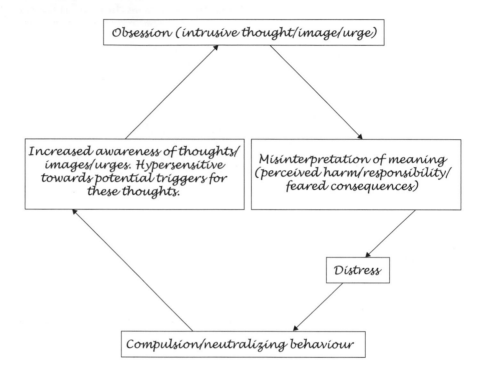

Looking at the model above, consider some of your own thoughts and behaviour and complete the CBT for OCD model for yourself. Work through the model using an example obsession that you struggle with and how this makes you feel.

Index